THE A–Z OF PUNISHMENT
AND TORTURE

THE A–Z OF PUNISHMENT AND TORTURE

Irene Thompson

Book Guild Publishing
Sussex, England

First published in Great Britain in 2008 by
Book Guild Publishing
Pavilion View
19 New Road
Brighton
East Sussex
BN1 1UF

Typesetting in Palatino by
IML Typographers, Birkenhead, Merseyside

Printed in Great Britain by
Biddles Ltd., King's Lynn

A catalogue record for this book is available from
The British Library.

ISBN 978 1 84624 203 8

Contents

Introduction

It's unlikely there's a single person who hasn't experienced punishment firsthand during their lives, whether it was only a gentle chastisement from a guiding parent or the wrath of an outraged headmaster or boss.

Punishment, in all its guises, has been, and still is, an intrinsic part of all societies and its history is long and colourful, not to mention extremely painful.

While the focus of this book is punishment, it is impossible to cover the subject fully without including torture and execution.

Torture could be administered as a punishment which resulted in death. Execution could be part of a punishment, and punishments imposed by courts of law often involved lengthy torture before ultimate death. The lines blur or overlap.

Man has punished wrongdoers since the dawn of time but at certain stages of history, he has demonstrated a frightening capacity for inflicting the utmost excesses of barbarity.

Walking his dogs one morning, George Buchanan was seized by his enemies and bound to a tree trunk. For the next 14 hours, on the hour, the attackers stabbed him with a knife in various parts of his body, making sure none of the wounds was fatal.

Eventually, they cut his throat and cut out his tongue. The man's four dogs were also killed and one of their tongues was put into the dead man's mouth and his into one of theirs. Not content with this unspeakable cruelty, they repeated the gruesome exchange of organs with the man's innards.

This was 17th century Scotland and even worse atrocities were also being perpetrated in Ireland at that time.

There is little to equal the savagery of the Irish papists during the wave of terror which swept the country in 1642. Protestant men, women and children were literally butchered or boiled, tortured and mutilated. Wives were forced to hang their own husbands, mothers to drown their own children and girls to murder their own parents.

We seemed to have progressed little since 621 BC, when the Greek lawmaker Draco wrote the laws of ancient Athens. They were so severe, they were described as having been 'written in blood' because all crimes became punishable by death. We still use the word Draconian to mean cruel or drastic.

The Romans put people to death for all

manner of crimes including writing rude songs or raucous behaviour in the street.

The advent of Christianity did little to staunch the flow of blood. During the reign of Tiberius from AD14, hideous cruelties were inflicted on his subjects, including forcing children to kill their parents before being slaughtered themselves. His successors, Caligula and Nero, were even worse.

From the Middle Ages to the 19th century, the death sentence was handed out for more than 200 offences, many of which were minor, such as cutting down a tree and robbing a rabbit warren. It seemed the simplest way to deal with wrongdoers and was intended to be a deterrent to others. Limbs were chopped off and bodies mutilated for the most trifling offence.

In medieval Europe, it was believed that the truth was revealed through the body rather than the mind, so only by torturing the body could the truth be unlocked.

There was also a law which stated that a confession must be given before a conviction could be made and torture was an effective way of extracting an admission of guilt, whether it was true or not. It wasn't until the 1700s that official torture began to die out.

Throughout this book are references to

Inquisitions. These were the manic hunts to root out first heretics – people whose views did not agree with the prevailing religious or political beliefs – then witches. They were instigated mainly by the Roman Catholic Church whose wealthy, corrupt and immoral leaders were despised by those who followed a pious Christian life. Fearing the growing opposition from non-Catholics, the 11th century Pope Gregory IX introduced the death penalty for heretics, which unleashed an orgy of tortures and killings by the inquisitors. These were monks who travelled throughout Europe finding offenders who they handed over to civil authorities for punishment. This kept their own hands free of blood.

The tortures devised by the inquisitors were remarkable in their ingenuity and sadism, usually employing implements to increase the suffering.

Victims either died during the torture, in prison or at the stake. Even if they did renounce their faith to embrace Catholicism, it wouldn't necessarily save their life. They had to give the names of their 'associates' before being thrown into a jail to rot unless they could afford an exorbitant fine.

By the 15th century, the inquisitors had turned their attention to witches. The persecutions began in Europe and continued, intermittently, until the 17th century.

The fever didn't reach England until the reign of Elizabeth I and, contrary to the familiar images, most English witches were hanged rather than being burned. Under the law, burning was the penalty for heresy, treason, which included murdering their husbands, and counterfeiting coins. Estimates for the number of women executed as witches during this dreadful chapter in history varies wildly from thousands to millions. It's believed around 100,000 witches were burned at the stake in Germany alone. In England, 1,000 were hanged, the largest group of which was 19 witches in Chelmsford in 1645.

Historian W.H. Hudson commented on the obvious pleasure power-mad judges took in handing out the sternest of sentences for the most trivial offences such as stealing a loaf of bread.

On one day in 1825, there were 170 cases to be heard at the Old Bailey and the worst crime was sheep-stealing. The death sentence was given to a man who stole a few shillings and an 18-year-old was sentenced to transportation for life because he stole a pocket handkerchief. 'It is surprising to find how very few the real crimes were in those days, despite the misery of the people,' wrote

Hudson. It wasn't until the late 1800s that the barbarity ceased and the focus shifted from punishment to rehabilitation.

The punishments of later centuries were mild compared with those in the Middle Ages. Convicts were transported to America or Australia instead of being executed, and gradually a prison system was introduced in the hope of rehabilitating offenders.

Although torture is illegal, the Torture Survivors' Network estimates that it is still used in 123 countries around the world.

While no one would elect to return to the dark days of excessive and unreasonable punishments, it's interesting to note that the worst discipline which can be imposed on an idle army recruit today is a 200-metre run, 15 sit-ups or 25 press-ups. It's a far cry from flogging.

ANIMALS

Amputation

Cutting off body parts as a method of punishment has been used for centuries.

In Roman times, Caligula delighted in inventing new ways to torture and punish people. He watched victims while he ate, claiming it improved his appetite, and once ordered a thief's hands to be cut off and hung around his neck so they dangled on his chest.

Though obviously too drastic for our modern Western world, amputation has to be acknowledged as an effective form of deterrent. After all, it's difficult to steal when you've had your hand cut off, and losing one's head cures all inclination to evil.

Some Muslim countries still impose the strict Shariah Islamic law which calls for a thief's hand to be amputated. Amnesty International estimates that 90 official amputations were carried out in Saudi Arabia between 1981 and 1999.

During the 1990s, thousands of Afghans regularly gathered in Kabul's sports stadium to witness the public punishments enforced by the Taliban extremists. Dol Agha, who was accused of being an informant for anti-Taliban rebels, was dragged into the centre of the stadium and forced to lie on his back. A soldier sat on top of him as his right hand

and left foot were amputated by a doctor whose face was hidden behind a surgical mask.

Beside 28-year-old Agha, the father of seven children, lay the right hands and left feet belonging to his friends, two of the hundreds of victims of this ghoulish punishment.

During Saddam Hussein's reign of terror, anyone heard criticising the regime had their ears amputated, according to records found by British army intelligence.

And in biblical 'eye-for-an-eye' fashion, a Saudi man who knocked out two of his friend's teeth during a fight had two of his own teeth extracted as punishment after the victim refused to pardon him. The attacker was jailed for a year for the offence, given several lashes and a fine. But the victim still wouldn't forgive him, which is an essential requirement under Saudi law in order to avoid physical retribution.

Great cruelties were inflicted on slaves during the 19th century. Many were hamstrung in order to prevent them running away, the tendon behind the knee being severed, which may account for the origin of the expression 'to be hamstrung'. Sometimes one leg was amputated if they had attempted to flee.

3

A slave in Mauritius in 1810 was punished for not fetching water sufficiently quickly by being flogged and then having seven of his teeth wrenched out with a pair of pincers. Another slave tried to run away and was captured, given 300 lashes and had his right ear cut off which he was then made to eat.

White people were rarely punished for the sickening acts of brutality and mutilation they performed on their slaves. In 1823, Madame Nayle of Flaco cut off her negress slave's nose and ears, tore out several teeth and was in the process of amputating her breasts when the poor slave died. No white person would give evidence in court and the evidence from other slaves was not heard. Madame Nayle was permitted to go free.

The most memorable modern amputation was performed in America by Lorena Bobbitt when she thought her husband had mistreated her. To punish him, she grabbed an eight-inch knife and sliced off his penis. The nation's manhood winced collectively as the news of the manicurist's handiwork swept through the nation in 1993. Thanks to medical wizardry, the 26-year-old Virginian restaurant employee with the appropriate name of John Wayne Bobbitt, was reunited with his sexual organ. His wife was found temporarily insane and spent three months in a psychiatric facility.

In another example of how far a scorned woman's fury will drive her, a Vietnamese woman living in Alaska cut off her man's penis and flushed it down the toilet to punish him for leaving her. Kim Tran, 35, then drove him to hospital, left him with a nurse and went home to clean up. Anchorage Water and Wastewater Utility workers pulled out the toilet and managed to retrieve the severed organ which was rushed to the hospital and reattached.

Thai women are notorious for punishing their men with penis amputation. More than 100 cases were reported in ten years, compared to one in Japan and two in Taiwan.

Rickshaw driver Prayoon Ekklang loved his beer and his bit-on-the-side in equal measure. When his wife discovered that the mistress was in town, she took the knife used to peel pineapples and put an end to his sexual activity forever. In a last act of vengeance, she tied the amputated penis to a helium balloon and sent it into the night sky, while her emasculated man slunk off to the nearest monastery to become a monk.

The final farewell to his manhood was only slightly less humiliating than that imposed on offenders in 16th century Rome who were forced to carry their severed testicles through the streets on a pole.

Animals

Several forms of punishment were named after animals – cat o'nine tails, 'horse-whipping' and 'kangaroo court', for example. Animals have been used in various ways to inflict punishment and death on humans.

Probably the best known is the persecution of Christians during the early Roman Empire when they were fed to lions or other hungry wild beasts in front of an ecstatic audience. The Romans hated the Christians because they refused to worship their gods.

Some viewed Christians as cannibals because they ate the 'flesh' and drank the 'blood' of Jesus during the communion. During the reign of the cruellest emperors, such as Nero, thousands of Christians were thrown into gladiator arenas to be mauled to death. Sometimes Nero would wrap Christians up in animal skins before throwing them to the starving animals then watch as the victims were torn apart. These grisly spectacles provided the equivalent of the commercial break during the gladiator fights which were the main entertainment.

Under Roman law, murdering a parent was regarded as the gravest possible offence because it violated the family unit and, therefore, the state. The punishment deemed to fit the crime was to be savagely beaten before being placed in a sack with a dog, a rooster, a poisonous snake and an ape and dropped into the nearest expanse of water. The victim would drown while the angry animals tore his flesh to shreds.

In a bizarre method of punishment and torture once used in Holland, and reminiscent of George Orwell's *1984*, the victim was tied to a table and a large metal bowl containing several rats was upturned and affixed to his stomach. Then a fire was lit on top of the container, sending the rodents into a burrowing frenzy to escape the heat. They literally gnawed their way through the victim's flesh and into his body. A similar method was used in Germany during the 17th century when a wild cat was tied to a prisoner's body and tormented until it used its claws and teeth to rip into his flesh.

The Tower of London housed a cell where prisoners were sent until they confessed to their crime. The floor was below high-water mark so it was flooded daily with foul water from the Thames. And the water brought a far greater horror – rats. The prisoners were forced to battle with the hordes of hungry rodents until, exhausted from sleep deprivation, they collapsed and succumbed to their horrible fate.

In Asia, crushing by elephant was a common sentence for over 4,000 years, especially for military deserters during the Roman Empire. A 19th century explorer to central India sketched a criminal being forced to place his head on a pedestal and being held there while an elephant crushed his head underfoot. The drawing was made into a woodcut and printed in a popular French travel magazine. Most Indian rajahs kept elephants to carry out executions by crushing and some of these animals weighed more than nine tons. Sometimes the public executions were prolonged either by dragging the victim through the streets attached to the elephant's leg, or by using an elephant trained to crush each limb, then the chest, with excruciating slowness.

In 1681, the English sailor, Robert Knox, described an execution he had witnessed in Sri Lanka in which the victim was torn to pieces by an elephant which had had iron spikes fitted on to its teeth.

Horses have also being corralled into

human punishment. We can all remember scenes in cowboy movies where the bad guy is trussed and dragged through the dusty streets behind a horse.

A more unusual use for the animals was employed during the Middle Ages when huge catapults were built to hurl long-dead horses into castles under siege. The starving and desperate defenders ate the putrid flesh and were quickly struck down with the plague.

Animals themselves were subjected to punishment in various parts of the world where it was believed that they were capable of committing crimes. In ancient Rome, an annual event was held commemorating the day their dogs slept through an enemy attack, leaving the geese to raise the alarm. To punish future canine generations for their negligence, bejewelled geese sitting on embroidered cushions and carried on elaborate litters were paraded through the streets alongside people holding up crucified dogs.

From the late Middle Ages to the 18th century, animals were, bizarrely, actually prosecuted and punished for their misdeeds. It's thought this odd idea stemmed from a passage in the Bible which says that an ox which fatally gores a human should be stoned to death. Lay courts handled crimes committed by domestic animals and the ecclesiastical courts dealt with wild creatures.

Cases of animal prosecution include:

- Rats taken to court in France for eating and destroying local barley.
- A French sow publicly executed after being tried and found guilty of infanticide. The pig, whose six other piglets were acquitted, was dressed in human clothes for her hanging.
- Franciscan friars in Brazil brought an action against ants which had burrowed beneath the foundation of their monastery, weakening the walls.
- A group of Parisian printer's apprentices staged a trial for the neighbourhood cats which had been keeping them awake at night with their yowling. The animals were found guilty and strung up on an improvised gallows.
- A 17th century Russian goat was exiled to Siberia for butting someone.
- A cock was burned at the stake in Basel, Switzerland, in 1474, for the crime of laying an egg, considered an unnatural event because they believed it would hatch into a monster.

- Other recorded crimes include homicide committed by bees, bulls, horses and snakes, as well as theft by foxes.

Asbos

Can you imagine what our ancestors would have thought of Asbos as a form of punishment? They would surely have seemed a remarkably easy option.

The Antisocial Behaviour Orders, introduced in Britain in 1999 as part of the Crime and Disorder Act, were intended to tackle the problem of nuisance neighbours.

Asbos have become widely used as a way to control tearaway kids who commit minor street crimes.

Though an Asbo is a civil order and a preventative measure, breaching one is a criminal offence carrying a maximum five-year jail sentence or a fine. Asbos have been widely criticised as ineffectual because penalties imposed are often ignored by the recipients.

In some parts of the country, every Asbo issued has been breached three times because yobs see them as 'badges of honour'. During 2005 in West Yorkshire, the 450 Asbos handed out by the courts were breached a staggering 1,301 times.

The Asbo has also been ridiculed for the silly ways it has been implemented.

- In 2004, a 14-year-old boy was banned from saying the word 'grass' until 2010.
- Pensioners in Chelmsford, Essex, were threatened with Asbos if they continued feeding pigeons in the town centre.
- Kent police attempted to fine Kurt Walker in February, 2006, for saying a four-letter word in a private conversation. Walker opted to go to court where the case was dropped.
- In Bristol, Zeroy Trought was given an Asbo for putting a sign in his pub's car park reading 'Porking Yard'. Police said this was sexually suggestive and religiously offensive as the pub was near a mosque.
- Oxford student Sam Brown made history when he was arrested for homophobic abuse of a police horse. When the revelling graduate drunkenly described the animal as 'gay', he was cuffed and thrown in jail by six officers. He was given an Asbo and a fine which he refused to pay and the subsequent court case was dropped due to lack of evidence.

BURNING

Banishment

When someone in a tight knit social or religious group refused to conform, banishment was a common way to punish them. Quakers, in particular, could be executed if they dared to return after having been banished.

The Amish banish from their community anyone who leaves their faith, and in strict Orthodox Jewish circles, families will treat a relative who marries outside the faith as having died, even observing the traditional mourning ceremonies.

Bastinado (or Falanga)

This Spanish word means beating the soles of the feet with a stick or similar implement. It's an effective punishment because there are clusters of nerve endings on the feet which rapidly transmit pain, and many small, fragile bones and tendons which can be injured. Sometimes the feet were tied together and strung up, or tied to a wooden plank. After the beating, offenders were made to walk around on their damaged feet, often carrying weights to increase the agony. The ancient punishment was used in the Inquisition, in China and in the Middle East where it's known by the Arabic word 'falaka'.

In the Middle Ages, it was often used to punish dishonest traders who tried to under sell. Bakers, in particular, were known for this, so many attempted to avoid official scrutiny with a goodwill gesture of giving customers 13 rolls for every dozen purchased. This is how the number came to be known as 'a baker's dozen'.

Beating

Corporal (to the body) punishment was banned in British schools in the 1980s, but, surprisingly, beating is still permitted in 28 American states, mainly in the religious 'Bible belt'.

Parents there believe that to spare the rod is to spoil the child and there is a widespread adherence to religions which teach that corporal punishment is not only acceptable but also necessary.

Beheading (see also Guillotine)

'Off with his head!' commanded the imperious and crazy Queen of Hearts in *Alice in Wonderland*. Perhaps if it was that easy to dispense justice, we wouldn't have so many criminals, or so many heads.

Decapitation with a sword or axe is usually a swift and sure method of execution though the head is technically still 'alive' for another seven or so seconds. It was the preferred method of execution for the nobility, who considered hanging only for the poor.

It was customary for the disembodied head to be parboiled and placed on a spike in a prominent location as a salutary warning to others. Sometimes dozens of heads were lined up at various London sites in gruesome rogues' galleries.

Among the first notable decapitations in history were Goliath in the Old Testament (David sliced off the giant's head after felling him with a stone) and John the Baptist, executed in the 1st century. John's 'crime' was telling King Herod it wasn't lawful for him to have married his brother's wife, Herodias. She resented this remark and was desperate to get revenge. When Herod held a birthday party, Herodias' daughter, Salome, performed a dance which delighted the king so much, he offered the girl anything she wished for. Her mother urged her to ask for John's head served on a platter, a request which Herod agreed to, albeit reluctantly.

Scots patriot, William Wallace, better known as Mel Gibson in the film *Braveheart*, was despatched at the behest of his arch-enemy King Edward I in 1305. Wallace was hanged, disembowelled and finally beheaded, just to make sure.

Perhaps the most widely known heads on the chopping block were King Henry VIII's two wives, Anne Boleyn and Catherine Howard, though their demise was decreed through Henry's whims rather than as punishment for any offence they had committed. During his 37-year reign, an astonishing 72,000 criminals were executed, many for minor offences.

Sir Walter Raleigh was sentenced to death by James I in 1618 for engaging in hostilities with the Spanish after the King forbade him. Raleigh refused to be blindfolded and touched the axe, saying: 'Doest thou think that I am afraid of it? This is that that will cure all sorrows.' He then instructed the executioner to 'Strike, man, strike!' But it took two blows to sever his head, which his wife embalmed and kept in a red leather bag until her death 29 years later.

Simon Fraser, the 11th Lord Lovat and a leader in Bonnie Prince Charlie's Jacobite Rebellion in England, has the dubious distinction of being the last Briton to be axed in 1747.

Executions as public events provided a mixture of entertainment and deterrent to the spectators who were mindful of the fact that the line between victim and onlooker was a fine one. In 18th century Germany the whole affair was conducted with great ritual and ceremony. After a public sentencing, the offender was taken to the scaffold in a procession of local dignitaries where religious ceremonies were performed. Priests intoned prayers, choirboys sang hymns and the condemned, if Catholic, confessed his sins.

In Protestant towns, epileptics brought glasses and mugs to catch blood from the severed neck which they drank as a cure for their affliction. Either the guillotine or the sword were used for the execution, depending on the custom of the region, and the proceedings concluded with a salutary sermon from the officiating priest or pastor.

Beheading was considered to be a humane, if gory, form of execution in the hands of a skilled headsman. However, one blow wasn't always sufficient to sever the neck – it took three attempts to remove the head of Mary Queen of Scots in 1587. The executioner couldn't believe his eyes when the Queen's little terrier dog ran out from beneath her voluminous skirts, yapping at him to stay away from his mistress's head.

In Europe, it was more common to use a sword for beheading. Though the blade was sharper than an axe, the head was not placed on a block which made it more difficult to make a clean severing. If the victim trembled or moved, the sword missed the neck and sliced into the body so the executioner had to try again. When a condemned prisoner in France volunteered to be an executioner to save his own skin, it took him 29 swings to remove the head of his victim.

John (Jack) Ketch, an executioner during the reign of King Charles II, became notorious for his inefficiency in a job where swiftness and accuracy were crucial.

After he'd beheaded Lord Russell in 1683, he apologised for missing his target because he was interrupted while taking aim. When he was about to top the Duke of Monmouth two years later, the Duke mentioned his predecessor, Russell, which made Ketch even more nervous. He had five goes with his axe before resorting to a knife to sever Monmouth's head from his shoulders. Ketch's name has entered folklore as a proverbial name for death or the devil, or as a name for the gallows.

Today, some countries still carry out beheadings and American hostages have become victims in recent years. In 2002, Daniel Pearl, a *Wall Street Journal* reporter, was kidnapped by terrorists in Pakistan, four months after 9/11. Despite the prayers of the world, along with his pregnant wife and family, 38-year-old Danny was executed by his captors.

Businessman Nicholas Berg was in the wrong place at the wrong time when he went to Iraq in May 2004, during the US-led occupation. The telecommunications worker was abducted and later beheaded by militants seeking revenge for alleged abuses of Iraqi prisoners. The decapitation received worldwide coverage because the horrific death was videotaped and released on the Internet.

A month later, Paul Marshall Johnson, a helicopter engineer living in Saudi Arabia, was taken hostage and executed as he was pinioned on a bed by three men. Again, the murder was captured on video tape. Johnson's head was found in a refrigerator in a villa in Riyadh.

Bilboes

Many punishments were contrived to publicly humiliate and degrade the culprit and the bilboes were one of the earliest of these. They're thought to have been imported from Bilbao, Spain, possibly on board the

Spanish Armada, for intended use on the many English prisoners they expected to capture on their arrival.

The bilboes were a simple contraption comprising a long bar of iron with two sliding shackles in which the offender's legs were padlocked. The weight of the bar alone prevented escape.

This easily transported instrument was used extensively on slaves in the West Indies and in America to punish erring colonists until it was displaced by stocks and pillories which could be built from the plentiful supply of wood there.

Birch

A traditional form of punishment in British schools was the birch, made from a bunch of lightweight birch branches. It was usually applied to the bare backside, causing intense smarting, and the level of pain increased with the number of lashes.

Dr. John Keane, Headmaster of Eton, is best remembered, not for his mastery of Latin, but for his dexterity at the flogging block.

On one evening in 1832, at the age of 60, he birched 80 sixth-formers in succession with unfettered zeal.

Boiling and Frying

When we think of humans being boiled, we tend to think of cannibals popping passing missionaries into a pot and cooking them for dinner. In fact, this appears to be purely mythical as there is no evidence that people were ever stewed whole in cauldrons. Cannibals much preferred to select the tastiest bits after the victim had been killed, in the same way we choose to eat our meat.

One reason for them not boiling whole humans may be simply that they didn't have the technology to make iron cauldrons large enough, except in South America where they did make them in clay. Another reason is that the cannibals wouldn't have wanted the contents of the internal organs and waste products polluting their people soup.

However, boiling prisoners was a legal punishment in olden times, right up to the 18th century. Life had far less value than it does today which meant that compassion, too, was in short supply, and man's capacity for revenge was boundless.

One of the most graphic descriptions was the torturing of the Maccabees, relating the torments and execution of a mother and her seven sons.

No horror movie maker could have come

up with such depravity involving racking, skinning, burning, amputation and, the final barbarity of having the tongue pulled out and fried. The mother, who had witnessed her sons' agonies, had her breasts ripped off before she was put into a red-hot frying pan.

Frying was an alternative to boiling and was conducted in much the same way as we fry our food today. The victim was placed in a large, shallow receptacle or dish containing oil, tallow or pitch, and fried alive.

Some of the earliest accounts of boiling come from China and Japan and a fictionalised description is included in James Clavell's novel *Shogun* where a European explorer is boiled alive after he's suspected of being a pirate or a spy.

During the Roman times, early Christians were often boiled to death for their beliefs, and in the Middle East, oil was used when there was a shortage of water, which made the suffering even more intolerable as oil has a much higher boiling point than water.

Boiling prisoners became a legal form of punishment in England in 1531, during the reign of Henry VIII when Richard Roose, a cook in the diocese of the Bishop of Rochester, was found guilty of poisoning seventeen people, two of whom died. He was sentenced to be boiled to death without the benefit of clergy, which meant he wasn't allowed to receive the usual special privileges due through his ecclesiastical connections.

In recent times, Idi Amin of Uganda and the government of Uzbekistan are alleged to have boiled a number of political dissidents. In 2002, a young Muslim prisoner, Muzafar Avazov, was boiled to death by the secret police in Uzbekistan. His mother, Fatima Mukhadirova, 63, managed to take some photos of her son's corpse which she sent to the British Embassy in a bid for justice. The Foreign Office sent them to the University of Glasgow where pathologists confirmed that Avazov had been tortured and immersed in boiling water. The Uzbek prison authorities claimed Avazov had died after inmates spilled hot tea on him. Two years later, Fatima was arrested and sentenced to six years hard labour in a maximum security jail, an imprisonment she wasn't expected to survive.

Boot

The boot, which came in a variety of styles, was a popular form of punishment and torture throughout England, Scotland and parts of Europe. The iron container in the shape of a boot encased the naked leg from foot to knee. Wedges of wood or metal were hammered in between the flesh and the side of the boot, lacerating the flesh and crushing the bones. The victim was invariably left a cripple.

The caspicaws was the Scottish equivalent of the Spanish boot and both men and women were subjected to its torments. The iron casing in which the leg and foot were contained had a screw attachment for compressing the calf. Sometimes the boot was placed in a movable furnace and as it got hotter and the agony intensified, the victims usually confessed whatever they were asked.

The brodequins, used commonly in Scotland during the 17th century, used boards placed around the leg and bound tightly with strong rope. Wedges of wood or metal were driven between the boards until the victim's flesh was torn and bones splintered or broken.

The Spanish boot was made of metal, and after the leg had been inserted, it was placed on hot coals and allowed to heat up, effectively roasting the victim's leg.

An alternative method was to pour boiling tar or liquid metals inside the boot, or the boot might be filled with cold water and slowly heated over a fire, causing the prisoner's leg to slowly boil inside.

The foot press clamped the victim's foot between two horizontal iron plates which were tightened in order to crush the foot. A crueller variation added sharp spikes on the plates which gouged the flesh, or a hole was bored through the foot as the plates were tightened.

An Englishwoman married to a Spaniard was charged with heresy in 1704 and sent to the Inquisition of Lisbon.

She was kept in a dungeon and fed on bread and water for nine-and-a-half months during which time she was whipped with knotted cords and burned on her breast with a red-hot iron. Steadfastly, she refused to admit the charge and was finally taken to the torture chamber again where she was tied to the chair. Her left foot was bared and an iron slipper, which had been heated in the fire, was fixed to her naked foot and left until the flesh burned to the bone. After a severe flogging, she was threatened with the red-hot slipper on her right foot but, unable to endure further agony, she signed a confession.

Boring

Considering the punishment for blasphemy used to be to have one's tongue bored with a red hot needle or iron, it's surprising anyone uttered an uncivil word. The method was transported to the New World along with the settlers who imposed it at the drop of an aitch. One Virginia gentleman, who spoke ill of another, was condemned to have his tongue bored through with an awl and then to pass through a guard of 40 men who each beat him. In Maryland, the offender was bored and fined for the first offence, and then branded on the forehead for a second offence. Quakers, who were considered a threat to the established Church, suffered terribly when they arrived in the New World and frequently had their tongues bored through with a red-hot poker.

Brainwashing

The term 'brainwashing' is one of those wonderfully descriptive expressions which has become a part of our everyday language. We are 'brainwashed' by the media, influential peers, religious cults, television commercials, etc., the exposure to some of which may well be considered punishment in themselves.

Though the word didn't exist before 1950, the more sinister application of its meaning did exist under other descriptions such as 'coercive persuasion'. Enemies of the Soviet Union, for example, were subjected to this kind of treatment. The aim was to penetrate the minds of the victims in order to break down their resistance, leaving the brain 'washed' and receptive to propaganda.

After the establishment of the People's Republic of China, similar techniques were used on citizens to make them accept the new doctrine. To the Chinese way of thinking, anyone with capitalist values was a criminal of the republic and had to be punished and programmed until they were willing to accept the social order. The Chinese term for the methods they used translates as 'to wash the brain'.

The expression reached the United States in the 1950s during the Korean War when sleep deprivation and intense psychological manipulation were inflicted on prisoners to break them down. One benefit of this was that a prison full of compliant soldiers required fewer guards to control them, leaving more men free to fight. Interestingly, it was found that the effects of brainwashing did not last.

Although many American GI prisoners of war later defected to the Communists, most of those who were eventually repatriated reverted to their original beliefs.

Branding

Branding was a life-long sentence for offenders because they had to wear the mark of infamy seared into their body for all to see. The Romans branded runaway slaves with the letter F for *fugitive.* In medieval England, the hot iron was applied to the forehead or the inside of the left hand and the letters used denoted the crime involved – R for rogues and vagabonds, T for thieves, etc. Vagabonds caught begging were rounded up and, without any trial, branded with the letter R. Gypsies were treated as badly. For shop-lifting, the penalty was burning on the cheek under the eye, and for blasphemy, the tongue was bored through with a red-hot skewer.

Thieves were branded in open court on the thick part of their thumb with a red-hot iron. They would hold it up to show the judge, asking 'A fair mark, my lord?'

If the judge nodded, the criminal was released. If not, the branding was repeated.

With such a prominent advert for their

crime, it was impossible for anyone who had been branded to get employment so they were forced into a life of crime.

Branding was abolished in England in 1829.

Brazen Bull

One of the most common forms of punishment inflicted by the ancient Greeks was the brazen bull, a hollow construction made from brass, with a door in the side.

The victim was shut inside the bull and a fire was set underneath it, causing the man to be roasted alive. It was a favourite of the tyrant Phalaris, who devised a way to turn the prisoner's screams into a sound similar to the bellowing of an ox, thus not distressing those who feasted around this macabre spectacle. Legend holds that when the bull was opened, the victim's bones shone like jewels and were made into bracelets.

Phalaris commanded the inventor, Perillus of Athens, to make the smoke rise in clouds of aromatic incense to disguise the stench of burning flesh.

With the sadistic cruelty for which he was renowned, Phalaris ordered Perillus to get inside the bull and test out the sound system.

Then he slammed the door shut and had the fire lit beneath the bull so he could hear the inventor's screams.

Perillus was rescued before he died, but killed soon after. It is said that Phalaris himself perished inside the bull when he was overthrown by his enemies.

The Romans used this torture device to kill Christian martyrs including Saint Eustace, who was roasted alongside his wife and children by the Emperor Hadrian.

Burial

Being accidentally buried alive is a primitive fear for many people. Even George Washington made his staff promise not to bury him until he'd been dead for three days.

Burial was used as a punishment as far back as the Romans when a vestal virgin was entombed for violating her vows of celibacy. She was given some bread and water just in case she was really innocent and would be saved by the goddess Vesta. She wasn't.

Unrepentant murderers were buried alive in medieval Italy and the Russians buried women who had killed their husbands, their head left above ground to prolong the agony.

A variation on burying alive is being walled

in, which was practised in Germany and Switzerland. The victim was locked in a room and a solid wall was built in front of the door to make escape absolutely impossible. It's hard to imagine the mounting terror felt as the wall was slowly erected. One murderess who certainly earned her horrible death was Erzsebet Bathory, a niece of the King of Poland. In a bid to achieve eternal youth, she killed more than 600 women so she could bathe in their blood. She was walled up alive for her heinous crimes.

Burning

Since the dawn of civilisation, societies have disposed of their enemies or criminals by burning them. Burning as a punishment was mentioned in the Bible, and the Babylonians and Hebrews all used it for certain crimes. The Romans burned thousands of Christians, sometimes after binding them with oil-drenched ropes before setting them alight and throwing them into cauldrons of boiling oil or molten lead.

They even roasted Christians alive over hot coals, so great was their hatred of people who would not accept the Roman gods. Emperor Nero blamed the Christians for the great fire that devastated Rome in 64 AD and immediately began exacting his revenge in a killing spree. He rounded up Christians and crucified them, fed them to packs of ravenous dogs and doused them with tar and lit them to create human torches.

Burning was a favourite sentence for those found guilty of heresy during the days of the inquisitions and for nearly three hundred years, condemned witches were dragged to the stake and consumed by the flames. In England, witches were rarely burned alive, but 1,000 were hanged or strangled first, and then burned.

Nearly three hundred protestants, including half a dozen children, were burned during the five-year reign of Henry VIII's daughter, Mary, in most cases for the crime of following the Protestant faith. It's not surprising that she earned the name Bloody Mary.

Heresy and treason were punished in England by burning at the stake for women, and being hanged, drawn and quartered for men. Treason included such offences as counterfeiting money and 'coining' – clipping coins and using the pieces of silver and gold to melt down and make more coins — as well as murdering one's husband or mistress.

One of the earliest recorded burnings in England was in 1222 when a deacon of the church perished at Oxford for embracing the Jewish faith so he could marry a Jewess.

The history books record stomach-churning descriptions of the sight of a living person being slowly consumed by flames. For some, the suffering was lengthened by a badly-made fire or the wind blowing in the wrong direction.

One method was to pile the faggots around the base of the stake to which the victim was attached with chains or iron hoops. Alternatively, the condemned was tied to the stake and the faggots were heaped up around them, effectively shielding their sufferings from the onlookers.

When Phoebe Harris was convicted of counterfeiting coins in 1786, 20,000 people turned out to watch her being burned at Newgate, the first woman to die there. She was hanged first, as was the custom by then, and then fastened to the stake.

Burnings at Newgate gradually became more and more unpopular among the residents of what was a respectable London business area and the practice stopped in 1790.

During the Spanish Inquisition, more than 31,000 people were burned between 1480 to 1815. This method of punishment was favoured because it didn't involve shedding the victim's blood, which wasn't allowed under the prevailing Roman Catholic doctrine.

It also ensured that the condemned's soul was cleansed during the burning and that there was no body to take into the afterlife, which was a severe punishment in itself.

The Inquisition's first targets were Jews who claimed to have converted to Catholicism but who had reverted to their faith, and then the purge extended to all Jews. This was the time of the *auto-da-fé*, a large and elaborate ceremony which involved mass trials of heretics and which culminated in burning orgies to destroy any opposition to Catholicism. Often these 'acts of faith' were timed to coincide with important events, thus ensuring a turnout of the entire population to witness the proceedings.

The prisoners were paraded through the streets wearing a *san benito*, or penitential garment, and a pointed hat decorated with crosses, flames and devils. Each had a rope around the neck and carried a tallow candle as they processed to the town square and was given one last chance to admit the error of their ways. Those who repented and were prepared to die in the Catholic faith had the privilege of being strangled before they were burned. Those who refused to repent were burned alive.

To celebrate the wedding of Carlos II to Marie-Louise d'Orléans, 51 people were burned alive in Madrid during the 14-hour mass execution. The king himself set light to the first pyre.

The largest *auto-da-fé* was held in Mexico when 108 Jews perished in the flames.

Crimes were often minor, such as Fernando, a Protestant schoolmaster, who was burnt for teaching the principles of his faith to his pupils, and a carver was burned for defacing an image of the Virgin Mary.

In 1605, Johnne Jak was put to the stake for bestiality and burnt along with the mare, his partner in the crime.

Torture by fire was also used in Italy and Spain to extract confessions. The accused was secured in the stocks and the legs and feet well-greased with fat so that the soles were literally fried by the heat.

The famous English highwayman, Dick Turpin, forced a woman to sit on the fire in her own house until she disclosed the hiding place of her money.

Burning has also been used widely in modern tortures with the use of cigarettes, matches, soldering irons and boiling water applied to the skin.

C

CHAIN-GANG

Caning

Today's schoolboy could be forgiven for thinking that getting 'six of the best' would be something worth having. Previous generations of naughty youngsters knew too well that bad behaviour would result in a trip to the headmaster's office to be given half a dozen swift whacks on the backside with a cane.

Journalist Richard Gibbon recalled how he was made to wait 12 hours before his punishment when, as a 13-year-old student at Edinburgh's exclusive Fettes College, he was caught talking after lights out. After the agonising wait, he was frogmarched to the house prefects' room where the beating was administered. Though the scars faded in six weeks, Gibbon said the experience was a sobering reminder throughout his life that if he was caught doing something wrong, he had to expect punishment.

The cane was the chosen instrument in most English schools because it could impart a considerable sting, even through two or three layers of clothing. It was also effective because the springy pencil-thick rattan made contact with a relatively narrow area of flesh. The distinctive hissing sound as the cane swished through the air was terrifying for the victim as he anticipated the imminent pain.

While Scottish state schools tended to employ the tawse*, or leather strap, until it was banned, private schools more often used the cane.

In 1977, the *Scottish Daily Record* newspaper ran an article on a 17-year-old Fettes's pupil who was caned for under-age drinking. The editor presumably considered the event sufficiently newsworthy to be published in a national paper. The college's most famous pupil, Tony Blair, also received six of the best, from an exasperated Fettes housemaster who described him as the most difficult boy he'd ever had to deal with.

Though corporal punishment was banned in English state schools in 1987, opinion polls consistently show that the public would favour its return.

Under the headline 'Backing for a Whacking', a newspaper telephone poll in 1988 reported 92.5 per cent of calls urging the reintroduction of this discipline.

And when 18-year-old Michael Fay was sentenced to four months in jail and six lashes with a cane for vandalism in Singapore (see **Flogging**), his fellow Americans overwhelmingly supported the harsh punishment. Frustrated with the ever-increasing crime

* see **Tawse**

rate, and the inability of a criminal justice system to deal with it, they looked enviously at the success of Singapore's unflinching deterrents.

Ironically, a Korean immigrant living in America was sent to prison for two years in 2000 for caning her teenage stepdaughter because she wore loose blouses and torn jeans. Her friends and family said the mother was only practising a traditional method of discipline, but the jury convicted her of child cruelty.

While we in the West have softened our policies, other parts of the world are hardening theirs. As recently as 2005, Indonesia's Muslim province of Aceh officially implemented caning as a punishment. It will be used to uphold strict Islamic law by punishing individuals who spread beliefs other than Islam. For example, a Muslim who missed Friday prayers three times in a row would get three strokes of the cane.

Castration

Where the death penalty wasn't imposed, mutilation of some kind was a favourite alternative punishment. Compulsory castration has been used in all cultures for hundreds of years. It caused great agony, as well as a threat to life, especially in primitive societies where anaesthetics or surgical hygiene were unknown. In addition, the victim suffered psychological torture.

Castration was rarely used as an official punishment or torture in civilised countries and after World War II, it was used even less because of humanitarian concerns following the Holocaust.

Surprisingly and relatively unnoticed, four American states passed laws as recently as 1997 calling for the castration of sex offenders, either chemically or surgically. There are now powerful drugs which reversibly block testosterone production. The action in Florida, California, Montana and Texas was prompted by two prisoners who actually requested the treatment. Lawmakers argue that castration is effective in controlling persistent sex offenders because it removes their impulses, enabling them to be released without posing a danger to the public.

Studies support this belief – of the 700 Danish sex offenders castrated after many convictions, relapse rates dropped from up to 50 per cent to just two per cent.

Sex offenders who volunteer can be chemically castrated in the Czech Republic and Germany. Surgical castration is not the painful, mutilating procedure it once was. Now the orchidectomy, as it's called, is performed during day surgery under local anaesthetic. Each testicle is removed through a small scrotal incision similar to that made during a vasectomy.

Chain Gang

The image of prisoners chained together while they sing and work in unison is an indelible part of American history. Slaves were shackled together to prevent escape and put to work under the hot Southern skies. The chains, which could weigh 20 lbs or more, caused nasty shackle sores where the iron chafed against the skin, and gangrene and other infections were common.

In modern times, prisoner chain gangs provided a cheap workforce for the government while at the same time acting as a crime deterrent to those who saw them.

Though the use of chain gangs had largely declined by the 1950s, some US states have since re-introduced them – including chain gangs for women.

Children

Children were punished in the same way as adults until well into the 19th century.

They were whipped and hanged and tortured, as well as being transported. Though homeless and hungry, they would still be beaten for begging. It wasn't uncommon to see a woman dragged to the gallows with a baby at her breast and older children clinging to her skirts. After her execution, they were put into the care of the parish or, if old enough, put to work for anyone who'd take them. Many subsequently died after working day and night for a cruel master.

Crank

This was an alternative to the treadmill as a form of hard labour for male prisoners over 16 during the 19th century. Unlike the treadmill, which could be used to generate power to grind corn or pump water, the crank served no useful purpose whatsoever.

A small paddle in a box containing sand or gravel or other means of resistance had to be turned on average 12,000 times with a crank handle. With a resistance of up to 12 lbs, this was no mean feat for prisoners already weakened by a prison diet, especially if guards made them earn their meals by their performance on the crank.

A Royal Commission in 1870 discovered a jail in which one prisoner had eaten only nine meals in 21 days because he had failed to meet the targets imposed on him.

The crank was a futile and tedious occupation, especially if the prisoner was kept in solitary confinement. Occasionally, driven to the brink of insanity by the task, a prisoner would smash the dial plate which counted the revolutions of the crank.

All that did was to earn him extra punishment.

Fifteen-year-old Edward Andrews was sentenced to crank labour for stealing a few pounds of beef. When he was twice unable to fulfil his task, he was put on bread and water, but the third time, he smashed the clock attached to the machine and was put in the **Punishment Jacket** (see separate entry). Ten days later, he was found hanging in his cell.

Crucifixion

Artist Sebastian Horsley recalls the horrific moment when five-inch nails were driven through his hands in preparation for his crucifixion.

'It was awful – far worse than I had ever dared to imagine,' he said. 'The pain was overwhelming.' Mr Horsley, thought to be the first Westerner to take part in the ceremonies, paid £2,000 to be crucified in the Philippines during an annual Easter ritual.

Although his feet were supported by a platform and the bands around his wrists and arms took some of the weight, the pain was excruciating. Mr Horsley's body began to produce hallucinogens in order to cope, and as the cross was hoisted upright by a dozen men, he passed out, temporarily spared the memory of further agony.

He and the other volunteers had even submitted to the traditional scourging before-hand, when victims were lashed 39 times with a whip made from leather thongs which had balls of lead tied to the ends. These bit into the naked flesh, shredding the skin, tearing the muscle and bursting the arteries.

Few but the fanatically faithful would volunteer to be crucified. Scottish DJ Dominik Diamond had every intention of suffering in his spiritual quest to 'rediscover' God.

But when confronted with a set of four inch nails, a man with a hammer and a group of bleeding self-flagellants, the 37-year-old changed his mind. He was jeered by spectators as he was driven away from the Philippines village of San Pedro Cutud where mock crucifixions of penitents have taken place since the 17th century. One villager, Ruben Enaje, has been crucified 20 times, remaining on the cross for a few minutes in the scorching heat before being helped down.

Crucifixion was invented by the Persians between 300 and 400 BC and imported to Egypt and Carthage by Alexander the Great. The Romans used it as a means of execution and also as a way of dishonouring and humiliating prisoners, most of whom came from the lowest social classes. After death, they were denied the dignity of a proper burial and instead, their corpses were either left hanging to be devoured by vultures or thrown onto a rubbish dump where they were torn apart by dogs and hyenas. This explains why so little evidence of crucifixion victims has survived to tell us more about the practice.

Crucifixion is considered to be the most painful, lingering death ever devised. Our word 'excruciating' comes from the Latin verb to torture, *excruciare*, close to their word for crucify *cruciare*.

Of course, the most famous crucifixion ever was that of Jesus Christ. Before the actual act of crucifying, Jesus, a young man in good physical shape, was gradually broken by tortures inflicted on Him, according to Dr. Cahleen Shrier, an associate professor of biology and chemistry at Azusa Pacific University, California and a regular lecturer on the subject.

Recounting the events of the day, she tells how after the Passover celebration, Jesus took his disciples to Gethsemane to pray. He began to sweat drops of blood, caused by a rare medical condition known as hemohidrosis in which the blood vessels that feed the sweat glands break down during states of high anxiety and the blood released from them mixes with the sweat.

The condition made Jesus's skin very tender, adding to the agony of the scourging He received which left His back in ribbons of flesh and skin. Roman soldiers placed a crown of vicious thorns on His head which pierced His skin and caused copious bleeding. The robe they put on His back at first helped the blood to clot, but soon it was torn off, causing the bleeding to renew.

In this desperate state, Jesus was incapable of carrying the patibulum, the horizontal beam of the cross, to the site of crucifixion so Simon of Cyrene took it for Him. The popular image of Jesus carrying the whole cross is likely to be inaccurate since it was the custom for the condemned to take only the cross beam.

It's believed Jesus was made to lie down in order to be nailed to the cross so He was thrown into the dirt, opening his wounds again. Despite the classical depictions of Him on the cross with nails through His palms, most experts agree this is inaccurate as the weight of his body would have ripped the nails through the flesh of His hands. It's more likely the nails went through His wrists. There is no definitive evidence on whether the tapered iron spikes, seven to nine inches long, were put through both feet or just one nail hammered in to hold the feet together. What's certain is that they caused unimaginable pain from severed nerves. As the cross was lifted upright, His shoulders and elbows dislocated as they were wrenched apart.

Death from crucifixion took hours or days. Often the Romans broke the victim's legs, hastening death, but they didn't do this for Jesus, so great was their hatred and fear of Him. No one knows for sure what exactly killed Him and, of course, it's impossible to replicate all He endured.

Some victims died from asphyxiation and others from hypovolaemic shock, where the heart can't pump enough blood around the body. Death could also be caused by heart failure, a blood clot on the lungs, multiple trauma or dehydration. The agony was often intensified by the cruelty of the executioners – they prodded the body with pointed rods, forced sticks into the anal orifice or smeared the face with honey to attract insects.

Though re-enactments are still performed by Christians as an act of faith, crucifixion has also been used in modern times as a form of punishment. The Japanese used crucifixion in the 16th century – in 1597, 26 Christians were nailed to crosses at Nagasaki.

A version of crucifixion was also used as recently as the Second World War at Dachau during the Holocaust. Prisoners reported that victims were suspended from beams by their wrists, which were tied. They died within ten minutes if their feet were weighted down, and within an hour if they weren't.

During World War I, there was a rumour that German soldiers had crucified a Canadian soldier on a tree or barn door using bayonets or combat knives, and reports out of the Sudan claim hundreds, if not thousands, of Christians have been nailed to crude crosses in remote regions of the country.

In 1997, two killers were reported to have been crucified in the United Arab Emirates for murdering five people.

Perhaps because of the religious significance of crucifixion, it has been used as punishment in Northern Ireland. In 1996, 18-year-old Martin Doherty was handcuffed and gagged by a gang in Belfast, who drove metal spikes into his elbows and knees. His crime? Shoplifting. He was in a coma for three days and left with serious injuries. And in 2002, Harry McCarton was nailed to a stile by loyalists in South Belfast. When the *People* newspaper polled its readers in Northern Ireland, an incredible nine out of ten backed the crucifixion as a method of punishment.

Other famous crucifixions include:

- St Peter, who asked to be crucified upside down as he didn't feel worthy to die the same way as Jesus because he had let Him down three times.
- About 6,000 followers of Spartacus were crucified along the 200 km road between Capua and Rome around 71 BC as a warning to other would-be rebels.

DUCKING

Death by a Thousand Cuts

In modern parlance, this expression is used to describe the slow death of anything from a national institution or ailing industry, to an endangered species. To the Chinese, it was a very real and horrific method of execution during which the victim was tied to a pole before the executioner systematically sliced off parts of the body.

The method used in Ling Chi or 'lingering death' varied. In one, a collection of knives with the name of a part of the body written on each, was covered with a cloth. The executioner pulled out a knife at random, cutting off whatever area was indicated.

Relatives of the condemned used to bribe the executioner to find the 'heart' knife as soon as possible.

Though the details of such punishments are shrouded in myth and mystery, French soldiers did shoot a series of photographs in 1904 depicting in graphic detail the stages of prisoner Wang Weigin's slicing death on a Bejing street. The executioner carved the biceps and quadriceps before cutting off the right arm and leg, and finally decapitating what was left of the body. Ling Chi was officially prohibited in China in 1905.

The Western interpretation of Ling Chi was

'death by a thousand cuts' but this is believed to be a mistranslation from the Chinese or an exaggeration of their method of slicing.

The Japanese used a similar method known as 'execution of twenty one cuts'. The art of the executioner was to take twenty slices before the twenty-first stroke delivered the *coup de grâce*. An eye-witness account of the death of rebel chief, Mowung, records:

> With superhuman command of self, the unhappy Mowung bore silently the slow and deliberate slicing-off – first of his cheeks, then of his breasts, the muscles of upper and lower arms, the calves of his legs, etc., care being taken throughout to avoid touching any immediately vital part. Once only he murmured an entreaty that he might be killed outright – a request, of course, unheeded by men who took a savage pleasure in skilfully torturing their victim.

Death Penalty

Taking the life of someone who killed another was a legal and logical response for our ancestors. At certain times in our history, criminals were executed for far less than murder and with far less public outcry than there would be for killing animals today.

Until 1808, the death penalty was given in Britain for around 200 offences, including attempted suicide and being in the company of gypsies for one month.

Even children aged seven to fourteen were executed for minor crimes.

The concept of human rights was unknown and there would surely have been puzzlement over concerns that, for example, the electric chair might be uncomfortable while the condemned was dying. Their philosophy was that if someone committed a crime, why worry about how painful their punishment might be? By the mid-1800s, the number of capital crimes had been reduced to four – murder, treason, arson and piracy.

The death penalty has now been abolished in over half the countries in the world but it is still retained in 70 or so. According to Amnesty International, during 2003 at least 2,148 people were executed in 22 countries, including 53 children, and at least 5,186 people were sentenced to death in 53 countries. Most executions took place in China, Iran, Saudi Arabia and the USA. The main methods used were beheading, electrocution, hanging, lethal injection, shooting and stoning.

Decimation

Decimation, or removal of the tenth, was an extreme military discipline in the Roman army used for mutinous or cowardly soldiers. The men were divided into groups of ten and the soldiers drew lots to find out which unlucky soldier would be chosen. He was then stoned or clubbed to death by his comrades. The remaining soldiers were punished by having their ration switched from wheat to barley. As anyone could be eligible for execution, regardless of their rank, the threat of decimation went a long way to maintaining discipline.

Denailing

The least little paper cut can be painful, so imagine what it would feel like to have your nails wrenched out. This was a simple form of punishment used, effectively, to extract information or admissions of guilt from prisoners. The insertion of needles or splinters under the nails is one of the most ancient tortures on record.

Medieval German witch hunters used wooden skewers dipped in boiling sulphur to drive into the flesh beneath the toenails.

When each nail was loose, it was ripped out with pliers. Allied soldiers imprisoned in Japanese camps during World War II were commonly given the nail torture.

Disembowelling

When the ancient practice of hara-kiri is depicted in movies, the Japanese ritual suicide is regarded with a mixture of admiration and bemusement on the part of Western viewers.

A criminal or dishonoured man was allowed to take his life by ripping open his bowels with two swift, deep cuts in the form of a cross. It's hard to understand how anyone could self-inflict disembowelment as a punishment, but in the ancient Japanese code of honour, it's a privilege to be able to do so in order to avoid being shamed.

This dates back to the days of the Samurai warriors when they were required to kill themselves rather than fall into the enemy's hands.

In the ritualised form of the samurai hara-kiri, known as seppuku, an attendant or loyal comrade sometimes stood by to cut off the head swiftly after the belly was cut open in order to hasten death. Hari-Kiri was an act of bravery which preserved the warrior's honour which is why Japanese soldiers committed hara-kiri at the end of World War II.

Ducking

Today's equivalent of a 'common scold' is your nuisance neighbour, the loud-mouthed woman who picks a fight with everyone and argues noisily and offensively.

From Saxon times to the 19th century, she would have been tied to a stool and unceremoniously ducked into the local pond or river to cool her ire.

> There stands, my friend, in yonder pool,
> An engine call'd a ducking-stool;
> By legal pow'r commanded down,
> The joy and terror of the town.
> If jarring females kindle strife ...

wrote poet Benjamin West in 1780.

Though principally reserved for females, brewers and bakers who gave short measures were also given a dunking, though for them it was called a 'cucking-stool'. The two names eventually came to mean the same thing.

One of the more unusual cases involved an unfortunate British merchant Capt William

57

Smith who drew the wrath of the folks of Norfolk, Virginia when he accused an American ship owner of smuggling. Already angered by the imposition of new stamp duties by the British, the crowd turned on Smith, bound him to a cart and stoned him. Then he was dragged to the wharf where he was tarred and feathered and taken to the ducking-stool. Smith was dragged through the town and lashed to the stool again amid yells from the mob for him to be drowned. Though saved from death by the Virginia militia, Smith's final indignity was to be thrown into a local river. He fled back to England.

Ducking was rarely fatal, unless the water was frozen or the engine – a type of wooden gallows construction – broke with the victim's weight.

The punishment was not only entertaining for the crowds, but also enabled justice to be seen to be done. Sometimes, the stool was designed to expose the victim's bare buttocks, which were an obvious invitation to missile throwers.

In 1770, a husband and wife were ducked together at Kirby, Yorkshire, after the magistrate decided their quarrelsome natures were as bad as each other's.

The ducking-stool was last used in England

in the early 1800s, but the offence of being a common scold stayed on the statute books until 1967. The last recorded case was brought in America in 1971 when a housewife was charged after an argument with her neighbours over a parked car. The Superior Court threw the case out.

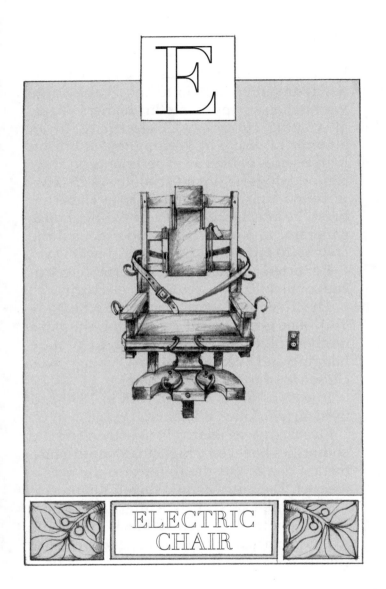

ELECTRIC
CHAIR

Electric Chair

While Thomas Edison was tinkering with his newly-invented light bulb, his rival, George Westinghouse, was promoting higher voltage, alternating current (AC) electricity. In an attempt to discredit Westinghouse, Edison held a series of bizarre experiments on stray cats and dogs he'd paid schoolboys 25 cents to round up. To the delight of a slavering press, he attached a 1,000 volt Westinghouse generator to a metal plate and executed the animals to prove how deadly the power was.

Reporters coined a new term 'electro-cution' to describe execution by electricity.

The inventors' work coincided with New York State Government's search for a humane method of capital punishment to replace hanging and eventually the AC voltage was chosen for the first electric chair.

It was installed in New York in 1890 and used on wife killer, William Kemmler.

Electricity was relatively new then and the authorities believed a high dose would cause instant death, but the first execution was a disaster. The initial charge singed Kemmler's flesh but he was still alive after 17 seconds. It took another 70-second shock to end his life as horrified witnesses gagged from the stench.

'They would have done better with an axe,' commented one.

When the first death row was built in New Jersey in 1907, the electric chair was reportedly designed 'with comfort in mind' to give the prisoner 'at least a comfortable seat in which to die.'

Though the technique for electrocution improved, Dr Harold Hillman, a neuro-biologist and expert on capital punishment, reckons that only stoning involves lengthier suffering than the electric chair. One prisoner needed five charges of electricity and several minutes in the chair before he died. Another, 17-year-old Willie Francis, didn't die at all after being given the maximum charge. Though he was temporarily reprieved, he was executed a year later. There have been some ghastly botches during electrocutions which have caused flames to billow from the condemned's head, creating acrid smoke and the smell of burning flesh.

When gangster George Appel was being strapped into the electric chair, he joked to watching newsmen: 'Well, folks. You'll soon see a baked Appel.'

Electrocution has largely been replaced by lethal injection in most American states.

Electric Shock

Captain Kirk and his Star Trek crew wouldn't have left their space ship home without their trusty phasers, which could stun their enemies unconscious. Sadly, truth is stranger than sci-fi and this type of futuristic weapon is now commonplace in more than 60 countries.

Amnesty International has expressed concern at the growing use of stun guns, stun belts and 'tasers', which fire a length of wire with darts at the end which attach to the victim's body or clothing to deliver an electric shock. Though intended to subdue or apprehend criminals, these readily-available weapons are widely used to torture or punish. The advantage of using an electric shock is that it can usually be inflicted without leaving bruises or scars. It can, however, leave the victim with permanent psychological or internal damage.

The American prison service uses stun belts in place of shackles to prevent escapes *en route* to court hearings. When activated, they deliver an eight-second 50,000-volt shock which causes the wearer intense pain, and their use has been criticised as being too open to abuse by some prison officers.

American police officers in 4,000 departments routinely use stun guns or 'tasers' to immobilise fleeing suspects, and British police have been using them since 2003. Figures for the number of deaths they have caused vary from 40 to 70, depending on who's producing the statistics.

An American dad was arrested after he used a 100,000-volt stun gun to discipline his eight-year-old stepson. Theodore E. Moody used the gun when the boy overslept and missed the school bus. He made the child walk to school while he followed, zapping his buttocks when the boy dawdled.

Another US couple used dog control techniques on their 17-year-old daughter. They punished her with a shock collar used to train pets, and kept zapping her until the battery ran out, a court in Mauston, Wisconsin, heard at the trial of the girl's mother and stepfather in 2004.

A few years earlier, a Californian man was given electric shock treatment as a punishment because he talked too much in court. Ronnie Hawkins, who faced 25 years in prison for persistent theft, kept interrupting Judge Joan Comparet-Cassini during his sentencing hearing. Hawkins was fitted with a four-inch wide electric waistband and given an eight-second shock. Witnesses said he grimaced and turned 'as stiff as a board'.

Perhaps based on the knowledge that low voltage electric fences can deter roaming cattle, bosses of Germany's Cologne Cathedral wanted the 'Wipe Your Feet' sign outside the building swapped for wires which would emit electric shocks when people stepped inside without wiping their shoes.

Exile

Politicians today would jump at the opportunity to vote for who they'd like to send into exile for their political crimes. Once a year, members of the ancient Athenian city assembly could do just that to get rid of a public figure. They wrote the name of the person they thought should be exiled on a shard of pottery (*ostrakon*) and put these into an urn. If 6,000 or more votes were cast, the named man was sent to another country for up to 10 years.

High-ranking citizens escaped capital punishment by volunteering to be exiled, though they might have their assets seized and be stripped of citizenship. Being exiled was a harsh punishment as it often removed husbands and fathers from their families and caused untold heartache, as well as penury, for all concerned.

In 1492, Spain threw out from its country all the Jews who refused to convert to Catholicism. They were given four months to sell their possessions and go, but they were forbidden from taking any gold or silver with them. Though many converted to the faith rather than giving up their wealth, up to 100,000 fled to other parts of Europe.

Every schoolchild once knew the palindrome Able Was I Ere I Saw Elba, which reads the same forwards and backwards. Fewer knew where Elba was and why it was famous. Emperor Napoleon Bonaparte lived on this island located off the north west coast of Italy during his first exile after his defeat at Waterloo.

He returned to France but was exiled a second time to St Helena, an isolated island in the South Atlantic, where he died in 1815.

Among other famous people who have been forced to leave their country, either voluntarily or otherwise, are Edward VIII who left England after giving up the throne to be with a divorced American, Wallace Simpson, and the Dalai Lama, spiritual leader of Tibet. When China occupied that country in 1951, thousands of Tibetans fled to India to form a government in exile.

Russia solved the problem of what to do with dissidents and criminals by sending them into remote regions of Siberia. Under the repressive Soviet Union regime, millions of people were rounded up and sent to live in exile in remote villages where many thousands died of starvation, cold, and overwork. The government did this because they feared that certain nationalities would turn against them during the impending World War II so entire categories of population were exiled, some for political or religious reasons, others for their ethnic background in a measure we now call 'ethnic cleansing'. Though there was a degree of freedom within the new settlements, the residents were forbidden from travelling beyond the immediate area.

FLOGGING

Fines and Forfeits

While the Courts of Assize and Quarter Sessions dealt with serious crimes, local courts dished out fines for minor offences, just as they do today. However, it's not likely that the local worthy who produced a lousy play at the annual pageant would be fined for contempt, as happened to Alderman Richard Trollop in 1520, according to records from Beverley, Yorkshire. Or that anyone would be fined for drying oats on the sabbath.

Fines were good business for the Archbishop of York who appointed the justices and received all the money they collected.

The Quakers were, unwittingly, a good source of revenue too. Described in a 1657 law passed in Massachusetts, USA, as 'that cursed sect', anyone found recruiting a new member had to forfeit £100. If found entertaining a Quaker, the forfeit was forty shillings. Worse, should a Quaker who had been whipped and banished, as the law required, have the temerity to return to the area, the men forfeited their ears.

Until 1870, anyone convicted of serious offences such as treason and murder would have their property forfeited, often leaving the offender penniless. The law today punishes wrongdoers with forfeiture, though

70

in much less drastic ways, such as taking away driving licences for road offences and personal possessions for debt.

Firing Squad (also Shooting)

A young soldier named Alfred, still suffering from shell shock and wounds, was discharged from hospital to fight alongside his brother, Arthur, in the 1916 Somme offensive. Within days, Alfred saw his beloved brother blown to smithereens in front of his eyes. Shaken to the core, he ran away but was found, court-martialled and shot as a deserter. Alfred was one of the 306 British soldiers who were executed for cowardice and desertion in the First World War.

After living with the stigma for 90 years, their families were told in 2006 that their loved ones would be given a posthumous pardon by the government. Death by firing squad was reserved for military personnel as it was considered a more honourable death than hanging, and was used only in times of war or armed insurrection.

Australian soldiers Harry 'Breaker' Morant and Peter Handcock were shot by a British firing squad in 1902 for alleged war crimes during the Boer War, though the fairness of their trial has since been questioned. Morant's famous last words were: 'Shoot straight, you bastards.'

During both World Wars, war criminals and spies were shot in the Tower of London.

Executions by firing squad became the most popular form of capital punishment in the 20th century with 86 countries using the method.

Vietnam started looking into alternatives to firing squads because the six mainly volunteer riflemen doing the job kept trembling and missing their target, leaving the commander to administer the fatal shot – the *coup de grâce* – with a handgun.

Shamed singer Gary Glitter avoided a shooting sentence in Vietnam for having sex with a 12-year-old girl by handing over several thousand dollars.

Uniquely, Thailand used a machine gun to despatch culprits until it started using lethal injections instead.

Many hundreds of soldiers were shot by firing squads during the American Civil War. In modern times, the death penalty was reintroduced in 1976 and a year later in Utah, murderer Gary Gilmore was shot at his request instead of being hanged. Six volunteers aimed their rifles at his heart and fired. In the traditional manner, one gun contained blanks so no one knew who had fired the fatal shot, though experts are able to feel the difference in the recoil.

The only other recent execution by firing squad in America was child killer John Taylor in 1996, an event which attracted 150 television crews from around the world.

The only US state to use a firing squad is Utah where the tradition is rooted in Mormon custom which holds that blood must be shed to punish a murder.

Execution by a single shot to the head is still a common form of capital punishment, especially in Communist countries, and 69 countries used it as a lawful method of execution up to the year 2000.

Though death penalty statistics in China are a closely guarded secret, they do carry out more death sentences than the rest of the world put together. In 2001, an incredible 1,781 executions were carried out using a bullet in the heart or back of the head for which the victim's family had to pay. Lethal injection is gradually replacing shooting executions in China.

Flagellation

Flagellation has a more religious connotation

than flogging and was originally a punishment meted out to erring monks. It also became a self-inflicted punishment in which penitents whipped their own backs, particularly during religious rites.

The Jews restricted the punishment to 40 strokes, but delivered only 39 just in case they'd miscounted and broken the strict Mosaic law.

The Romans, however, used flagellation widely and set no limit on the number of lashes which could be given. Not surprisingly, this meant that many victims died during or after the beating.

The flagellum was made from oxhide thongs, knotted or weighted with slivers of bone, metal balls or hooks.

There was actually a flagellant movement during the 13th century and bands of bare-backed beaters travelled around Europe exhorting the sinful public to repent.

The practice is still seen in some countries where Catholics re-enact the Easter story and flagellants, often wearing crowns of thorns, lash their backs until they bleed.

During the Inquisition, heretics could sometimes escape being burned at the stake by subjecting themselves to a beating by the priest during the Sunday Mass. Every fourth Sunday afterwards, the penitent had to visit every house where he had met other heretics and be whipped at each one. If the inquisitors left town without releasing the penitent, the poor man faced a lifetime of monthly scourging.

Flaying

The gruesome practice of removing the skin from a body is deeply rooted in history.

In Viking times, flaying was the standard revenge on Saxons who committed rape. With pitiless precision, the offender's body would be cut and peeled until the skin had been separated in one piece. Then, with the blood still dripping, it would be nailed on a chapel wall.

The Assyrians also flayed the skin from captured enemies and nailed them to the city wall as a warning to anyone else who attempted to defy their rule, while the Mexican Aztecs skinned victims of ritual human sacrifice.

With tongue firmly planted in his cheek, Jonathan Swift wrote 'Last week I saw a woman flay'd, and you will hardly believe how much it alter'd her person for the worse.'

Revellers at a 2005 Dutch carnival laughed at the man in the strange costume as he mingled for hours with the jostling crowds. They were aghast to discover later that the unusual covering was in fact the skin of the 42-year-old man's mother who he had flayed. Her body was found in their apartment in the southern town of Vlaardinge.

Flogging (also Whipping)

An unobtrusive gravestone in a London cemetery marks the passing of a young soldier, a private in the Queen's Own Hussars. There seems nothing surprising about such a death, except that 27-year-old Frederick John White was flogged to death in 1847 for being drunk and disorderly, 25 years after a law made it illegal to beat donkeys and horses. Private White was given 150 lashes for a relatively minor offence and died 26 days later. The previous year, 659 British soldiers were whipped with the cat-o'nine-tails, used commonly for military punishment.

Flogging was authorised by the Mutiny Act of 1689 as a method of punishment in the British Army. At first they used sticks, the birch or the flat side of a sword blade. In the early 18th century, the cat-o'nine-tails appeared, so called because there were nine separate thongs of whipcord, each knotted in three places. This vicious implement tore the flesh off the bones of the victims and often killed them.

In the navy, flogging was carried out by the bosun's mate. A new cat, which was heavier than the army version, was made for each flogging from a two-foot length of sturdy rope with nine 'tails' or pieces of rope attached to it. Once made, it was put into a red baize bag until needed.

The whip, which could break a piece of wood in half, inflicted the most savage injuries on a man's flesh. The offender was generally lashed to an upturned grating and the punishment witnessed by the entire crew. If more than a dozen lashes had been ordered, the second bosun's mate would take over. The most severe form of flogging was 'round the fleet' during which the number of lashes given was divided by the number of ships in port and the offender was rowed between ships to receive his punishment.

The Romans were the first to flog people in public. Criminals were tied to the back of a cart and whipped all the way through the town to the place of execution, a practice which continued for centuries. Their slaves were flogged mercilessly too, and it wasn't uncommon for the whipper to collapse from exhaustion before he'd finished his job.

Before the advent of the prison system, some method of punishing wrongdoers had to be devised, whether it was for men, women, children or those in the armed forces.

In order to shame, as well as to punish, an offender, whippings were usually done outside and in England almost every town and village had a whipping-post, often combined with a pillory. Sometimes the culprit was tied to the back of a cart, stripped to the waist and whipped as he was paraded through the streets in the ancient manner.

Women were not spared this punishment though their crimes were likely to be related to prostitution, such as keeping a disorderly house. An unusual case involved Mary Hamilton who was whipped through the town for dressing as a man and marrying 14 women.

With the dissolution of the monasteries and other religious houses, thousands of vagrants who had taken shelter in them, plus thousands more labourers who had worked in them, were thrown on to the streets. Their numbers added to the already huge poverty problem throughout the country which is why they were treated so badly.

The Whipping Act of Henry VIII (1530) stated that vagrants were to be tied, naked, to the back of a cart and pulled through the streets of the town while being beaten with whips until their backs were bloody. Then they were sent packing to their town of origin.

One of the cruellest whipping sentences was handed out to Titus Oates, the informer, in the reign of James II. In addition to being pilloried twice, he was flogged from Aldgate to Newgate and after a two-day break, from Newgate to Tyburn. An eye-witness claimed Oates received around 2,000 lashes.

In 1807, the number of lashes was restricted to 1,000, and then to 50. English social reformer Jeremy Bentham was concerned with the inconsistency of flogging. He reasoned that 20 lashes given by a small, sympathetic man would have vastly different results from the same number of lashes administered by a strong, mean man. To resolve the discrepancy, Bentham proposed the use of a flogging machine which would lash every offender with equal force. He never made Entrepeneur of the Year for, as practical as his ingenious invention was, it was never manufactured.

Though flogging died out in England towards the end of the 18th century, the practice continued in the colonies – on slaves in particular – and in the British army and navy for another 100 years.

The origin of the expression 'there's no room to swing a cat' is the fact that it was almost impossible to stand upright between the decks of old wooden battleships, so floggings had to take place on deck.

Since convicts who had been transported to Australia were already 'imprisoned' for their crimes, the only way to further punish them was by flogging with a whip or cat- o'-nine-tails. They were suspended by the hands beneath a tripod of wooden beams, known as the triangle, and a doctor or medical worker stood by to check the fitness of the prisoner during the beating. If he fainted or suffered excessive injury from the whip, the punishment was postponed until he had healed enough to receive the remainder of strokes to which he'd been sentenced. This was usually between 20 and 100 strokes, though it has been known for prisoners to receive more than 3,000 strokes over a number of months. Flogged men proudly 'showed their stripes' – whipping scars – as a mark of their manliness.

In Jamaica, slaveholders could hire people to whip their slaves. The 'common whipman' was employed by the parish and his services could be bought by the plantation owners.

Flogging is still used as a form of punishment in some countries. In Singapore it's imposed for about 30 crimes from begging to drug trafficking.

The six-lash sentence imposed on 18-year-old American, Michael Fay, in 1994 for spray-painting two cars, provoked international outrage. An appeal from President Bill Clinton succeeded in reducing the sentence to four lashes. Fay escaped lightly by local standards – a boy convicted of the same crime a week earlier received 12 lashes. Flogging is also widely used as punishment in countries like Iran and Saudi Arabia.

Foot Roasting

The Romans extracted information from prisoners by heating flat plates of iron until they were red-hot, then applying them to the soles of their victim.

This was also one of the most popular methods of torture during the Spanish Inquisition. The prisoner's bare feet were coated with fat and confined in stocks. Then they were slowly barbequed over red-hot coals

G

GIBBET

Gallows or Gibbet

In the late 15th century, Halifax grew from a tiny Yorkshire hamlet to a 500-strong community, thanks to the emerging cloth trade. Bolts of manufactured cloth were delivered to the town where they were washed in the clear spring water, then stretched out on wooden frames and left to dry in the open air on the surrounding hillsides. As the price of cloth increased, so did the number of thefts. The town's gentlemen were reluctant to become hangmen but the problem was solved with the invention of a machine which would cut off heads without the intervention of human hands. The town was granted the 'privilege of the gibbet' from the Crown and the primitive construction erected in the market square, ready for the weekly spectacle attended by Saturday shoppers.

This gibbet was a simple wooden frame inside which a block of wood was attached to a cord and a pulley so it could be moved up and down. A sharp iron axe, weighted with lead, was fixed to this block. When the offender placed his head beneath the axe, the cord was released and the blade swiftly removed the head.

In fact, it was severed with such force, the

head often went flying into the crowd of startled onlookers and one bounced into the wicker basket of a woman riding by on her horse. Rumour has it that the teeth seized her apron and wouldn't let go.

The only hope for the gibbet victim was to withdraw his or her head before the blade fell and then run like the wind.

A man named Dinnis is reputed to have done just this, even stopping en route to answer queries from passersby whether Dinnis was being executed that day with a ribald: 'I trow not', a response which became a common local expression.

The only other man to escape was John Lacy in 1623 who made the fatal mistake of returning seven years later, believing he had been pardoned for his crime. He was executed without trial but earned the dubious honour of having *The Running Man* pub named after him.

The Halifax gibbet was the immediate predecessor to the guillotine but, though it worked well for individual executions, it would have been too slow for multiple beheadings.

Though frequently used as a synonym or a substitute for the gallows, the gibbet usually describes the upright beam with a horizontal arm from which bodies were suspended after execution. They were either wrapped in chains or encased in a full body iron framework. Sometimes they were suspended alive and left to die when they could be given to surgeons to be dissected.

In 1775, an Irishman named Matthew Cocklain was hanged for murder and gibbeted in Derby. On Christmas Eve, ten months after the body was suspended, a group of friends sharing a few seasonal drinks at a tavern bet each other that no one would dare to go near the gibbet. One brave soul took his Dutch courage in his hands and agreed to take a basin of broth out to Cocklain. In the depths of the dark, cold winter night he carried a ladder and the bowl of soup to the foot of the gibbet and climbed the ladder. When he lifted the bowl to Cocklain's mouth, saying, 'Sup, Matthew,' he heard a voice reply, 'It's hot.' The man threw the soup over the body and fled, terror-stricken, back to the hostelry to claim his well-earned winnings from the friend, the corpse's voice, who admitted he had spoken from his hiding place behind the gibbet post.

North country highwayman John Whitfield was gibbeted alive near Carlisle where he hung for several days in agony until a mail coach driver, unable to bear the heartrending cries, put Whitfield out of his misery by shooting him.

The day Lincolnshire wife killer Tom Otter's corpse was hung in chains, the townsfolk celebrated with a week of merry making. Several years later, the flesh around his jaw bones had fallen away, leaving a cavity in which a bird decided to build her nest. The arrival of nine baby birds prompted the composition of a rhythm still remembered in the area:

'There were nine tongues within the head
The tenth went out to seek some bread,
To feed the living in the dead.'

The custom of hanging bodies in chains was abolished in 1834.

Garrotte

It was a nifty little device for the sophisticated double agent. A piece of knotted cord tightened around the neck could dispose of an enemy swiftly, silently and cleanly.

The first recorded use of the garrotte or strangling cord was in ancient China in a form of execution known as the 'bow-string'. The prisoner was tied to an upright post with two holes bored in it through which the ends of a cord from a long bow were passed.

These were pulled tight round the neck by the executioner until the condemned was strangled.

Garrotting was used during the Middle Ages in Spain and Portugal and it was sometimes used in England to execute religious heretics before they were burned at the stake.

By 1828, the metal version of the garrotte was the standard method of execution for civilians in Spain, replacing hanging, and remained so until 1974.

With the Spanish garrotte, a rope was put round the prisoner's neck and the post, and the rope was then tightened by the executioner twisting a stick in it.

More than 700 people, including 16 women, were executed in the 19th century with one of the most 'hands on' execution methods in modern history. It was later modified to kill the prisoner using a spike or blade thrust into the neck to sever the spinal column, which was swifter and more certain, though no less distasteful.

Andorra was the last country in the world to abolish the death penalty by garrotting in 1990.

Gas Chamber

When the gas chamber was invented, it was thought to be a humane method of capital punishment. Opinions rapidly changed when it was discovered death could take up to 15 minutes.

In America, nearly a thousand prisoners were put to death in the gas chamber between 1930 and 1980 when it was the legal method of execution in 11 states. But it's considered to be one of the cruellest methods as prisoners suffer violent and painful convulsions for many minutes before they eventually die.

The prisoner is taken to an airtight chamber where he or she is strapped into the chair. At a signal, pellets of sodium cyanide are dropped into a container of sulphuric acid located in an adjacent room, releasing deadly hydrogen cyanide gas through holes in the chair. The average time to kill a human is 9.3 minutes. Prisoners are advised not to hold their breath as this only prolongs the inevitable inhalation of the lethal gases.

One of the most graphic portrayals of a condemned prisoner's experience was in the movie *I Want To Live*, based on the case of Californian mother of three, Barbara Graham. She went to the San Quentin gas chamber on 3 June 1955 for a violent murder many believe she didn't commit. She refused a last meal with the bitter words: 'Why waste good food on me?'

Twice on her last morning the execution was delayed, briefly raising her hopes of a reprieve. It never came.

Most of America's gas chambers were built in the 1920s and are now old and unsafe – any leaks in the seals could prove fatal for staff and witnesses. Since replacing each one would cost a huge amount of money, it's cheaper to use lethal injection.

Millions perished in the Nazi gas chambers during World War II. Their crime: being either Jewish or physically or mentally disabled.

Long before those dark days, it's believed that more than 100,000 black slaves were gassed during Napoleon's regime when they rebelled in Haiti and Guadeloupe.

Sometimes ships' holds were used for mass executions when sulphur, easily available from local volcanoes, was burned to give off a toxic gas. The revelation appeared in the book *The Crime of Napoleon* by Claude Ribbe who said officers unwilling to take part in the killings had left written accounts of events.

Gouging

In his play *Oedipus Rex* the Greek playwright Sophocles tells the tragic story of the eponymous hero who gouges out his own eyes when he discovers he has unwittingly killed his father and married his mother.

Though no one today is likely to impose such a drastic punishment on themselves, it can still be carried under strict Islamic law, upholding the principle of, literally, 'an eye for an eye'.

When the late Robin Cook was Foreign Secretary, he saw a 50-minute tape, smuggled out of Iran, showing a doctor removing a prisoner's eyes while the man screamed and moaned in agony.

In 2002, a 21-year-old Iranian woman was sentenced to have both her eyes gouged out in public for blinding a man with acid powder when he tried to rape her at gunpoint.

But in 2005, Amnesty International was instrumental in saving an Iranian man from an eye-gouging sentence after the Iranian Supreme Court had rejected his appeal.

A few years ago, Indian vigilantes carried out their own punishments on more than 20 petty criminals by gouging out their eyes and pouring acid into the empty sockets.

Two unemployed youngsters caught

stealing a bicycle were pinned down and blinded in broad daylight, their screams going unheeded by witnesses.

Guillotine

Across the Channel in France, heads began rolling all over the place in 1792 with the invention of the guillotine, a development of a machine originally used as early as 1307. Ironically, it was devised as an alternative to the barbaric and protracted punishments meted out at the time, especially to the lower classes who were either hanged or broken on a wheel.

Dr Joseph Guillotin, a humanitarian, wanted to find a swift and simple method of execution which would be relatively painless to the condemned. The structure was designed by Dr Antoine Louis who used the English gibbets as inspiration. The final contraption comprised a blade, fitted with a 65 lb iron weight, mounted between two wooden posts.

A crescent-shaped neck strap held the victim's head in place. The Paris executioner who practised on corpses and live animals declared it a perfect device for the job.

During the peak of its use during the French

Revolution, the guillotine was topping 60 or more people a day with its distinctive slanting knife blade. There was hardly time for the blood to dry. In fact, there was so much blood, it gathered in pools at the base of the scaffold and flowed over the cobbled streets in red rivers.

The only people who expressed disappointment with the new method of execution were the crowds who felt shortchanged with such a swift despatch of heads.

Louis XVI and Marie-Antoinette were two of its most famous victims. The glamorous and extravagant Queen of France, who adored expensive jewels and fancy dresses, ended up in an undignified heap in the cemetery, her head lying beside her body, awaiting the gravediggers.

Rumours claim that the woman who later became Madame Tussaud took the opportunity of sculpting a wax model of the head as it lay ignominiously on the ground. Madame Tussaud developed her skills creating death masks of famous people who had been beheaded. These were transformed into wax models and the rest, as they say, is history.

Guillotines became fashionable in a variety of ways. Miniature replicas were sold to cut cigars at modish dinner parties or as children's toys, complete with live birds on which to practise, while women wore earrings in the shape of miniature guillotines.

Guillotines were also used in other countries, including Germany, where up to 45 machines were thought to have been employed. In 1942-43, the Nazis guillotined 20,000 political dissidents, more people than were beheaded during the French Revolution.

The last recorded use of the guillotine was in France in 1977 and it was abolished in 1981.

H

HURLING

Hanging (see also Gallows and Gibbet)

A raucous, jeering crowd of three thousand or more drank their way to the grandstand where ringside seats fetched high prices for the entertainment. A football match? No. A prisoner's two-hour journey from London's Newgate Prison to the gallows at Tyburn in the 1700s, which resembled a rowdy carnival combined with a pub crawl. The condemned sat in a horse-drawn cart, often on his own coffin, as the procession edged towards the scaffold. One of the stopping places was the hospital of St Giles in the Fields where the prisoner received 'a cup of charity'.

Hanging was the usual method of execution in England for all but the gentry as far back as the Anglo-Saxons. One 18th century earl begged the judge to sentence him to beheading rather than hanging but his pleas were rejected, as was his request for a silken rope. The only way he could retain his dignity was wear a white suit, embroidered with silver, and to be transported to the gallows in a carriage drawn by six horses.

Today, we often use pubs as landmarks when giving directions. In the Middle Ages, they used the location of the gallows or gibbet, known as road marks, to guide travellers.

In the 18th century, London was known as the City of the Gallows, and probably the best known hanging site was Tyburn in London, near where Marble Arch stands now. Here the condemned were originally hanged from the boughs of several elm trees, the first execution documented in 1196.

In later centuries, the banks of the River Thames were lined with gibbets from which hung rotting remains encased in chains as an ongoing reminder to miscreants. Sometimes the gallows were carried around the town and suspects hanged on the spot.

People were often hanged for trivial offences, such as a young mother, with a baby at her breast who was hanged for stealing a shilling's worth of lace.

Nor were children exempt from the severe punishments handed out by the 17th and 18th century courts. Twelve-year-old William Jennings was sentenced to death for breaking into a house, while in 1708 a seven-year-old boy and his eleven-year-old sister were hanged in King's Lynn, Norfolk, for theft.

The local press didn't regard the execution of two children as worth reporting, but the incredible survival of a Scottish mother kept the gossips busy for months. Despite her vehement denials, Margaret Dickson was sentenced to hang in Edinburgh for the murder of her newborn baby. After the execution, she was cut down by friends who put her in a coffin and set off home. While they were having a drink on the way, one of them screamed in terror as he saw the lid of the coffin being slowly raised. They plucked up the courage to investigate and when they lifted off the lid, Margaret Dickson sat bolt upright. After a good night's sleep, she went home where she made a full recovery.

Hanging as a punishment in England is thought to date from the Saxon period when victims were simply suspended from a tree branch with a piece of rope round their necks and left to die by slow strangulation.

Later, the condemned was made to climb a ladder which was pushed away once the noose was in place. However, the drop wasn't sufficient to guarantee instant death.

In the 17th century, a cart replaced the ladder and when the prisoner was strung up, the horse was made to gallop off, leaving the victim dangling. It improved the chances of a quick death, especially if the executioner helped by pulling the legs of the poor wretch to tighten the noose. However, on more than one occasion, when bodies had been seized from the gallows and sold for dissection as the law decreed, the victim was found to be alive just as he was about to be cut up.

It wasn't until the addition of a hangman's knot and the introduction of a vertical drop over a trapdoor that a broken neck was assured. Unfortunately, the jerk on the rope was sometimes so strong, the victim was totally decapitated. The method was eventually refined to vary the drop according to the weight of the victim.

Making sure the prisoner actually died was one problem. Another was making sure the hangman was sober enough to fulfil his duties. The *Derby Mercury* newspaper of 6 April 1738, reported that the executioner hired to despatch two burglars was so drunk, he thought there were three prisoners and tried to put the noose around the parson's neck too.

Being an executioner wasn't a bad job in the 18th century. Since more than 200 offences carried the death penalty, there was always plenty of work and they got to keep the victim's clothing. They were well-paid and not only received tips from their wealthy clients but also took backhanders from surgeons wanting to buy the bodies for dissection.

There was also an active market in the sale of the thumb and finger bones from thieves' hands. The reasoning was that since they had taken more than their share of worldly goods before they'd been caught and hanged, their digits were believed to be lucky and likely to go on acquiring goods for the new owner.

In addition to the unseemly post-hanging scramble for the body and bits, the deceased was also set upon by gaggles of women trying to clutch the lifeless hands. They were covered in 'death sweat' which the women rubbed over their own cheeks, breasts or the bodies of their children in the belief that it would cure warts, acne and other unsightly skin conditions, as well as tuberculosis.

One woman even undid her blouse so the dead man's hand could be placed on her breast. Mothers brought their children to the gibbet to stroke the dead hand and ensure themselves a long and healthy life, and barren women came in the hope that a touch of the hand would enable them to conceive.

One hangman was reported to charge two shillings and sixpence ($12\frac{1}{2}$p) to touch the corpse or to buy a piece of the rope for luck.

The last British hangings were in 1964, nine years after Ruth Ellis became the last women to take the hangman's noose for shooting her philandering lover.

Our most famous hangman was Albert Pierrepoint, who was the most prolific execu-tioner of the 20th century. Though a precise figure has never been released, it's estimated that between 1932 and 1956, he hanged 433 men and 17 women. That figure included around 200 Nazis after World War II. Albert came from a Yorkshire family which provided three of the country's chief executioners.

Perhaps the most unusual executioner was an Irish woman named Betty, who once lived in abject poverty with her young son. When he grew up, he emigrated to America to make his fortune. One night in 1780, a well-dressed stranger knocked on Betty's door asking for food and shelter.

She took him in, but while he slept, she killed him and stole his money. Looking through his wallet, she was horrified to discover she had murdered her own son.

Betty was condemned to death at Roscommon Jail but on the appointed day, the executioner was unwell. Seeing a chance to survive, she called out: 'Spare me, yer honour, and I'll hang'em all', which she did.

Lady Betty, as she came to be known, was appointed the jail's hangwoman where she remained for 30 years.

Japan is alone among the industrialised countries today in retaining hanging as capital punishment. In 2007, it set a 31-year record by carrying out ten hangings in ten months. Rising crime rates in some Caribbean islands are prompting the reintroduction of hanging.

Hanging, Drawing and Quartering

This was one of the most barbaric forms of punishment and execution. The victim was first dragged on a hurdle – a wooden panel – to the place of execution, hanged, then, while still alive, disembowelled and dismembered. After the genitalia and entrails had been removed and burned, and sometimes the heart removed, a stout rope was attached to the four limbs and secured to the harnesses of four horses. The animals were whipped simultaneously in opposite directions, wrenching the victim's limbs from their sockets. If this ghastly treatment didn't succeed in severing the limbs, the executioners chopped each joint with a hatchet until the limbs could be pulled from the trunk. The process could take hours. The head and four body parts, which may have been parboiled to preserve them, were put on public display to deter would-be traitors.

There is confusion about whether the 'drawing' referred to dragging the body to the place of execution or whether it meant removing the innards during the disembowelment.

The hangman had to ensure that the noose choked, but didn't kill, the victim, lest the agony end too soon.

In the 1500s, more than 100 Catholic martyrs were hanged, drawn and quartered for spiritual treason – failing to acknowledge the official religion.

While we may blanch at such atrocities, the diarist Samuel Pepys casually reports that on Saturday, 13 October 1660, he went to see Major General Thomas Harrison being hanged, drawn and quartered. Then Pepys took some friends out for an oyster lunch before returning home where he became annoyed at his wife's untidiness.

The last execution of this kind in France was that of Robert François Damiens in 1757 for the attempted assassination of Louis XV. The court ordered that Damiens be tied to a scaffold and burnt with pincers on his chest, arms, thighs and calves. His right hand, with which he was supposed to have committed the crime, was to be burnt in sulphur and boiling oil; melted lead, resin, and wax mixed with sulphur to be poured into his wounds. After that, he was to be dismembered by four horses and his remains burnt.

Damiens's agony went on for hours as each torture was applied. When the horses failed to disconnect the sinews between his body and his limbs, his body, still alive, was quartered with a knife.

His friend, the infamous Casanova, reports

that he 'watched the dreadful sight for four hours.

'I was several times obliged to turn away my face and to stop my ears as I heard his piercing shrieks, half his body having been torn from him.'

Gunpowder plotter, Guy Fawkes, and six of his accomplices also died from this cruel punishment, even though we commemorate his demise with bonfires. It remained lawful punishment for High Treason right up until 1870.

Hanging Judge

Though several lawmen have earned the soubriquet hanging judge, England's best known was George Jeffreys, lst Baron Jeffreys of Wem. He was appointed by James II to try those responsible for the Monmouth Rebellion of 1685 which tried to overthrow the unpopular Catholic king.

In the series of trials, known as the Bloody Assizes, Judge Jeffreys sentenced around 250 to hanging and another 800 to be sold as slaves in the colonies. The judge enjoyed attending executions and often sat at the *Prospect of Whitby* pub in Wapping to look across to Execution Dock where bodies

104

remained hanging until they had been washed by three tides.

Houses of Correction

In the late 1500s, London was the largest city in Europe with around 140,000 inhabitants. It was a tough life for the poor and homeless, especially since Henry VIII closed all the monasteries in the country, on which the destitute had relied for survival.

With this lifeline removed, the beggars and homeless appeared on the city streets, along with the thousands of labourers who had worked in the monasteries.

Their desperate plight alarmed and intimidated the wealthy who could no longer ignore this part of their society.

One of Henry's homes was Bridewell Palace in London which he rarely used. In 1550 his son, Edward VI, donated it as a refuge for the poor who had to earn their keep doing tedious chores that bordered on punishment, such as working the treadmills.

Authorities were obliged to open them around the country but the 200 Bridewells, as they came to be known, though established as workhouses, developed into Houses of

Correction as more and more criminals were sent to them from overcrowded prisons.

As a prison regime developed, the work became increasingly hard and the punishments more severe, despite the fact that the poor had committed no crime.

Whippings became a spectator sport with voyeurs paying to view the beatings.

Hulks

During the American War of Independence, English authorities had to stop the transportation of convicts. As there weren't enough prisons to house them all, they decided to use hulks, leaky old troop and slave transport vessels sitting idle on the Thames in London, on the Medway in Kent, and in Portsmouth and Plymouth.

It led to a dark and shameful chapter in the history of prison administration. Men, women and children, some as young as two, were held in truly horrible conditions, chained in darkness, filthy, diseased and abused.

New arrivals were sent down to the lowest deck to work their way upwards as prisoners died or completed their sentence. The former was more likely as conditions below were appalling. At times, each prisoner had only an 18 inch space in which to sleep and that area was shared with a huge population of rats. Lice were endemic and food scarce as the corrupt crew siphoned off most of the bread and meat intended for the prisoners, either selling it or eating it themselves. The convicts were forced to work onshore in arduous and dirty work, such as cleaning sewers and mining coal.

The most minor infringement of shipboard rules could earn them a flogging or a spell in the hell hole of solitary confinement.

At night, the violent, the insane and the dishonest were clapped in irons and confined below deck to live or die.

The 'temporary' solution to housing convicts lasted for 12 years and only a small proportion of them left the hulks alive, either as free men and women or in Australia, the new destination for transportees.

Hurling from a Height

In Ancient Rome, murderers or traitors were hurled to their death from a steep cliff known as the Tarpeian Rock. According to legend, the vestal virgin Tarpeia opened the gates of the city to admit the enemy Sabines, thinking they were bearing gifts. Instead, they crushed her to death with their shields and threw her from the rock which now bears her name.

Perillus, inventor of the brazen bull, was thrown from the Tarpeian Rock after being nearly roasted alive in his own creation.

During the reign of Francis I of France, criminals were made to fall from a height in order to break the limbs, a method known as *estrapade*. Then victims were left helpless until they literally starved to death. According to J.F. Millingen's *Curiosities of Medical Experience*, 1837, many 'actually devoured the flesh of their arms in the agonies of hunger and despair.'

I

IMPALEMENT

Impalement

The most gruesome methods of punishment or execution were often the simplest. Impalement, for example, required only a stake to cause a long and unimaginably painful death. There is evidence from carvings and statues that impalement was used in Ancient Persia and Ancient Greece – 3,000 Babylonians were impaled when the country was invaded by Darius I.

In 17th century Sweden, they used it as a death penalty for members of the resistance by inserting the stake between the victim's spine and the skin. It took four or five days for him to die. Usually the stake was secured in the ground with the victim attached. Sometimes it would be carefully inserted through the body, avoiding the heart, in order to prolong the dying process.

The most famous users of impalement were Ivan the Terrible and Vlad III Dracula, also known as Vlad the Impaler. Though steeped in legend, there is enough evidence to support stories of Vlad's cruelty, which was perpetrated on a grand scale.

One account claims he impaled an astonishing 30,000 people in a Transylvanian city. He liked to arrange his victims in geometric patterns – rings of concentric circles set around the edge of the city, for example, with the height of the stake indicating the rank of the victim. The corpses would be left to decay for months. Vlad enjoyed the killings so much, he held elaborate banquets in their midst while the victims died slowly around him.

It's not known for certain how much author Bram Stoker borrowed from Vlad's life for his eponymous character Dracula. It's likely that only the name and not the evil deeds were matched.

Russian ruler, Ivan the Terrible, was responsible for the murders of at least 30,000 men, women and children in his vengeance attacks on the city of Novgorod in 1570.

For five weeks, he ordered the most savage tortures and deaths to be carried out on the people he believed were traitors to the Czar, including plucking out ribs with red-hot irons, boiling, roasting and impaling victims.

Infecting

The story of how British soldiers wiped out native American populations by giving them blankets infected with smallpox may provide colourful material for the screenwriters and novelists, but historians doubt it ever happened. In exchanges of letters between Lord Jeffrey Amherst, commanding general of British forces in North America in the late 18th century, and Colonel Henry Bouquet, the idea was certainly discussed. However, there is no evidence that the plan was actually carried out.

There is little doubt, however, about the ability of vindictive lovers to pass on the AIDS virus, the punishment for most of whom is simply to die of the disease themselves. In 2003, Mohammed Dica, a father of three, became the first person in 137 years to be successfully prosecuted in England and Wales for transmitting a sexual disease.

The Inner London Crown Court jury returned unanimous guilty verdicts on two counts of 'biological' grievous bodily harm on two of Dica's lovers.

In a similar case in 2004, a one-legged German sex tourist infected hundreds of Thai girls with the AIDS virus because 'they were bad'. Though police there believe wealthy Hans-Otto Schiemann deliberately had unprotected sex with as many as 500 women, they were powerless to prosecute him. Schiemann waged his hate campaign to punish Thai girls because he believed they were responsible for infecting him and his wife with the disease. 'What he did was the

same as murder,' said Sommart Troy of the
Thai AIDS Group.

Iron Gauntlet

Despite the name, this method of torture,
often used in the Tower of London,
comprised iron rings which were placed
around the prisoner's wrists and gradually
tightened with a screw. The prisoner was
made to stand on a stool while the chains
were attached to an overhead beam and then
to the wrists. When the stool was removed,
the victim was suspended in the air, his whole
weight pressing on his wrists where the metal
gauntlets cut into his flesh.

One prisoner recounts how his arms
swelled until the flesh covered the gauntlets.
He fainted and when he came round, the
torturers were replacing the stool to support
his weight until he recovered. Then they
removed it and let him hang again, on and off
for five excruciating hours.

Iron Maiden

This horrific killing device is shrouded in
legend and Hollywood mystique. Sometimes

the life-sized figure would be painted with the face of Virgin Mary and mechanical arms would reach out to the victim. Once in her embrace, spikes would emerge to impale the body. It was a long and lingering death over several days, with the victim bleeding to death or dying of asphyxiation. The device was so thick that no screams could be heard from the outside once the doors were closed.

Sometimes prisoners were starved for weeks beforehand, and paraded through the streets being whipped by members of the public, leaving them weak and wounded before their worst ordeal had begun.

The most famous of these dreadful devices was the Iron Maiden of Nuremberg, which was about seven feet tall and three feet wide, with double doors. Inside, dozens of sharp spikes were fitted which could be moved to skewer the desired organs of differing sized victims.

The Iron Maiden has made many appearances in films and books. Kurt Vonnegut describes her in *Slaughterhouse-Five* and Roald Dahl's novel *Matilda* mentions a similar device called the Chokey. Fans of the Addams Family will recall an Iron Maiden in their spooky home and Johnny Depp's character in *Sleepy Hollow* found his mother's corpse inside an Iron Maiden.

Irons

Prisoners thrown into jails during the 18th century could expect to be confined in body irons and left for months on end, unable to move. Sometimes there would be a collar on the neck, a large ring for the waist and two rings for the ankles, which were connected by the heavy links of the chains. The weight of all this iron meant prisoners couldn't stand upright and they suffered intolerably from being permanently crouched.

To add to the injustice, prisoners were actually charged for use of the irons, as well as for admission to the jail, the bed, food, candles, plates and, if they were lucky, coals for heat. Those too poor to pay were thrown into the rat-infested pauper's side of the prison where conditions were abysmal. Those with money could pay for lighter chains. Either way, once the fetters had been riveted in place by a blacksmith, only the smith could remove them, unless the prisoner escaped and got others to file through them or knock out the rivets with a hammer.

JOUGS

117

Jougs

Teenagers who disobeyed their parents in 16th century Scotland could find themselves locked in an iron collar attached to the church door and left at the mercy of the jeering populace. The jougs, as this ancient punishment was known, was similar to the stocks and used mainly in the north of England and in Scotland to discipline members of the clergy or minor offenders. The culprit was padlocked in the hinged collar which was chained to a public building.

In Tudor England, children were brought up very strictly and weren't even allowed to sit down in front of their parents without express permission. Any child showing lack of manners or respect was harshly punished in front of the whole town by being put in the jougs, as was anyone who failed to attend church.

John Persene was brought before the magistrates in 1651 accused of missing church for five weeks. He was sentenced to be publicly rebuked and locked in the jougs if he missed more than two sabbaths ever again.

Alternative spelling of the words – 'juggs' or 'joggs' – suggest it gave rise to the slang name for prison, the 'jug'.

KEELHAULING

Kangaroo Court

Sham courts are held by those who have taken the law into their own hands and usually mete out harsh punishments. No one is exactly sure how the name arose but it could have originated during the Californian Gold Rush when, because of the transient nature of life then, it was necessary to proceed from accusation to punishment 'by leaps', with or without a proper court hearing.

Another explanation is that roving judges were paid on the basis of how many trials they conducted and their salary could depend on the fines they extracted from the defendants they convicted. They were seen as hopping around the country, trying as many cases as they could in the shortest possible time, giving them the image of kangaroos.

There's also the possible derivation from the informal courts held to deal with 'claim jumpers', or simply because there were so many Australians in the area looking for gold.

Keelhauling

Any poor sailor subjected to this punishment was unlikely to survive. He would be tied to a rope which stretched under the ship's hull, thrown over one side and dragged under the keel to the other side. A gun was fired during the process, not only to frighten the victim but also as a warning to the rest of fleet to behave themselves. The more drastic form of the punishment was to drag the victim from the bow to the stern of the ship which was invariably fatal.

Either way, hulls tended to be covered in barnacles and marine growth which could rip open the flesh horribly. If that didn't polish off the sailor, drowning usually did.

Believed to have been devised by the Dutch navy, the word 'keelhauling' derives from their word *kielhalen* which means 'to drag along'. Though it wasn't an official punishment in the British Royal Navy, there are many reports of it being used in the service, as well as among pirates.

Kneecapping

Kneecapping was a widely-used punishment during the Troubles in Northern Ireland, to some extent replacing the messier method of tarring and feathering. In the late 1970s and early 1980s, there were so many incidents, surgeons at the Royal Victoria Hospital in Belfast developed specialist techniques for treating the injuries caused by knee-capping.

Variations of the punishment, used by both Protestants and Catholics, were inflicted according to the perceived offence. Most victims were shot in the thigh as a warning but 'repeat offenders' could get a 'six pack' – shots fired into the kneecaps, ankles and elbows. Major arteries were severed and kneecaps blown off completely.

Many victims claimed compensation and received payments of several thousand pounds for bone damage and complications. Ten per cent of the estimated 700 cases seen by the hospital had to have their legs amputated and many never fully recovered the use of their legs.

Kneecapping can also be administered by hammering the joint, as happened to collaborators in the Philippines after the Japanese invasion, or by using an electric drill. Power tools have also been used by East Timorese militants to slice through prisoners' bones.

LYNCHING

123

Labour Camps

During the oppressive years of the Soviet Union, millions of political prisoners and other criminals were sent to the notoriously brutal labour camps in the depths of Siberia, Russia and the Soviet Far East. Here they toiled in temperatures as low as minus 60°C building the Trans-Siberian Railway or working on the roads. In their cramped quarters, they were issued with just one blanket. The unimaginably vast network of penal camps ultimately comprised 476 complexes housing up to 15 million prisoners.

The Kolyma site alone covered an area six times the size of France and contained more than 100 camps where an estimated three million prisoners died between 1931 and 1953.

The Marble Gulag in Siberia, which is dwarfed by 8,000 feet high granite mountains, has been turned into a museum which allows Westerners to visit for the first time.

During the three years it operated, 83 prisoners made a bid for freedom up the vertical rock face. None made it.

Novelist Alexander Solzhenitsyn, who spent eight years in the Gulag, won the Nobel Prize for literature in 1970 with his work *The*

Gulag Archipelago. It revealed for the first time the true story of what life was like for prisoners there.

Lethal Injection

In recent years, lethal injection has become the favoured method of despatching the condemned in America, where 37 states use it as their sole method or as an option.

In the only comparative study ever made on the suffering that accompanies execution, expert Dr Harold Hillman found that lethal injection is the least painful method of capital punishment, due, in part, to the fact that the cocktail of drugs administered to the prisoner contains a barbiturate along with the killing agent

While it might seem a challenging task to get personal feedback from the victims, Dr Hillman, a neurobiologist at the University of Surrey, studied the subject for nearly half a century before reaching his conclusion. It was based on observations of condemned prisoners, post-mortem examinations, physiological studies on animals and medical literature.

A few years ago, the ever-efficient Chinese introduced a fleet of mobile execution vehicles to help cover their vast country. The prisoner is strapped down on a metal bed in the back of the vehicle and the executioner presses a button to start the automatic injection process which can be viewed on a video monitor next to the driver's seat. Job done, the van sets off for the next drive-in death.

Lynching

Black labourer Melby Dotson fell asleep on a train journey through Baton Rouge, Louisiana. When his dream turned to a nightmare that he was being lynched, he began crying out in terror. Concerned the noise would disturb other passengers, the guard leaned over Dotson to shake him awake, but when Dotson saw the uniform, he thought his dream had become reality. Still half asleep, he pulled a gun from his pocket and fired, killing the guard instantly. Dotson was arrested at the next station but later that day, he was dragged from his cell and hanged from a telegraph pole. This the way they dispensed justice in the American Deep South in 1899.

The words 'lynch mob' struck terror into the hearts of black Americans who dared to challenge white supremacy. Slaves who tried to escape and those who helped them were prime targets for the lynch mob. More than 3,400 men and women were killed, mainly in the southern states, after the end of the Civil War. If the lynching was racially motivated, which most were, the victims were also mutilated or burned. The executions became almost a festive event in certain areas, and locals gathered with their picnics among the souvenir sellers as they were carried out. Yet the perpetrators were never identified. Neither eye-witnesses nor law officers would say they recognised anyone involved. The State and local governments did little to intervene and several times refused to pass anti-lynching legislation. In the western states, lynching was accepted as part of the pioneer justice and the lynchers knew they wouldn't be punished.

Lynchings continued in America until relatively recently. For example, in 1930, James Irwin was found guilty of murder in Georgia. A lynch mob chained him to a tree-trunk and systematically cut off his fingers and toes, then pulled his teeth out with pliers before setting him alight.

A year later, Raymond Gunn from Missouri was chained to the roof of the local schoolhouse, soaked with petrol and set alight while the baying mob watched him die.

People have been taking the law into their own hands for centuries but the expression 'Lynch law' is relatively recent, first recorded at the beginning of the 1800s.

No one is entirely sure who Lynch was. One contender was American William Lynch, who wrote Lynch's Law, an agreement with the Virginian authorities in 1782 allowing him to pursue and punish criminals in his area. However, he handed out only corporal punishments like flogging, and never lynched anyone. Over the years, Lynch Law came to mean the imposition of punishment by people operating outside any legal system, including hanging criminals without a trial.

The Ku Klux Klan , the white supremacist group, went on lynching blacks right up to the 1960s.

Lynching incidents have also been reported intermittently in various parts of the world, notable in the troubled areas of the Middle East.

MUTILATION

Mental Torture

Most tortures are designed to cause enough physical pain to reach the victim's mind, thereby achieving a confession or information. When the mind is the objective, the torture can result in a complete destruction of the victim's personality. A good example of this is in George Orwell's *1984* in which prisoners are taken into Room 101 to confront their deepest fears.

During the Stalin era, the Soviets used their new expertise in the emerging science of psychology to punish political prisoners. Dissidents were frequently sent to mental institutions for 'treatment' where they had to live among the criminally insane, sometimes for the rest of their lives. These buildings were often former prisons, with the bars still at the windows.

Inmates were given high doses of tranquillisers and experimented on with mind-altering chemicals. This, together with their constant proximity to the insane, usually sent them mad as well. The only hope of freedom was to acknowledge and support the Soviet political system.

In Victorian Britain, girls pregnant with illegitimate babies were frequently locked up in psychiatric units as punishment. When their baby was taken from them at birth, their grief, coupled with living among the deranged, often created mental problems which kept them confined for the rest of their lives.

Mutilation

While this subject is covered under specific headings, in general, the idea of mutilation was to inflict a permanent and public reminder of the offender's crime.

This could take any form the cruel and twisted minds of the judges could dream up, including amputation, eye-gouging or nose-splitting – or all three.

William the Conqueror brought the idea of mutilation from Europe when he invaded England in 1066, declaring it a more effective deterrent than hanging.

The Danes were particularly brutal, once slicing off the noses and cutting off the right hands of an entire crew of captured sailors. They believed that capital punishment was the easy option, preferring to inflict what they called 'gentle punishments' which, in addition to amputations, included plucking out the eyes or scalping.

Under Henry VIII's rule, ears were severed

simply for non-attendance at church, while thieves had their fingers chopped off.

William Prynne, a Member of Parliament, a barrister and a Puritan, received a life sentence in jail, a fine of £5,000, expulsion from the legal profession and the removal of his ears in the pillory for his crimes against the State. Three years later, the stumps of his ears were shorn off in the pillory and he was branded with the letters SL, meaning 'seditious libeller' (one who speaks out against the State). Sometimes the hapless pillory victims were left to wrench their own ears away from the board to which they had been nailed.

In France, removal of the tongue was a common punishment for blasphemy, and to induce Jews to hand over their money, their teeth were extracted.

Long hair and wigs had their uses in days when ear-cropping was commonplace. Still, many a sudden breeze or a romantic ruffle through the tresses revealed an ugly hole where an ear used to be or a branded letter on the forehead.

When an Elizabethan writer, named Stubbs, was punished for seditious libel by having his right hand chopped off with a cleaver and a mallet, he raised his hat in his left hand and said in a loud voice: 'God Save

The Queen'. The assembled multitude fell into a stunned silence.

Sometimes it was private individuals, not the State, who inflicted savagery on others. In the reign of Henry IV, a law was introduced to prosecute those who performed illegal maimings, known then as 'mayhems'.

The equivalent of our street gangs were the Mohocks, young men who established a reign of terror in London by slitting noses and attacking men and women as they walked the streets. The public retaliated by arming themselves with guns and setting up man-traps, but this was eventually banned because so many innocent people were injured or killed.

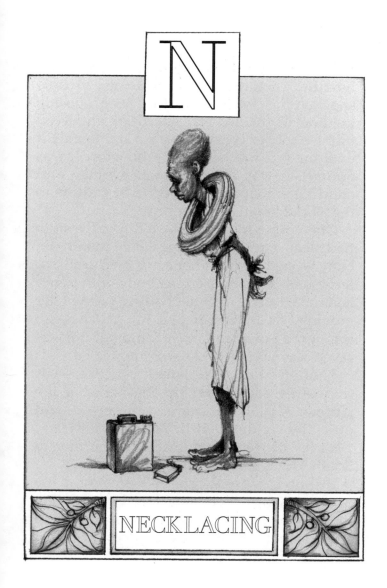

NECKLACING

Necklacing

During the apartheid regime in South Africa, horrific pictures of necklacing victims shocked the civilised world. This grotesque method of torture and execution involved filling a rubber tyre with petrol and forcing it over the victim's head or body before it was ignited. It was used on men, women and children who were believed to be traitors to the black liberation movement.

One young mother, married to a freedom party leader, recalled having her 10-month-old baby wrenched from her arms by a group of teenagers. They doused her body with petrol and forced a tyre over her body to prevent her moving. As they searched for matches, an armoured police car arrived and her life was saved seconds before she was immolated.

Though the gruesome practice was frequently carried out in the name of the African National Congress, the movement officially condemned it. Between 1984 and 1988, 706 blacks were murdered by burning in South Africa, 390 of them by 'necklacing'.

Bishop Desmond Tutu once saved the life of a man about to be necklaced by running into the crowd and throwing his arms around the prisoner. The mob were forced to retreat and abandon the killing.

Necklacing is also used on the island of Haiti to punish supporters of dictator Jean-Claude Duvalier. It's known as Père Lebrun (Father Lebrun) after a car parts dealer from whom the tyres are bought.

In Brazil, locals who inform on drug dealers have a tin barrel hung around their neck, instead of a tyre, which is filled with petrol and ignited.

Noise

An excess of noise can be a punishment in itself, especially as part of a torture regime.

Machines which generate intolerable 'white noise' are an acknowledged part of torture 'hardware' commonly employed.

Amnesty International has reports from prisoners who were subjected to the monotonous whine of machinery, such as a generator or compressor, for six or seven days. One man told them that he was driven to the brink of insanity by the noise and had tried to commit suicide by banging his head against metal piping in his cell.

In a re-creation of the interrogation experience of a detainee in the US-run Guantanamo Bay camp in Cuba, a journalist was subjected to white noise which sounded like a woman screaming, played backwards in a repetitive and inescapable drone for 51 hours. At the end of that time, he asked to quit the experience as he couldn't stand any more.

Closer to home, and a familiar problem for many, noisy neighbour Sharon McLoughlin was banned from owning a television, stereo or radio and ordered out of her Birmingham flat after tormenting residents with music and noise equivalent to the 65 decibel level of a passing train.

OAKUM
PICKING

Oakum Picking

When prisoners were sentenced to hard labour in the mid 1800s, one job they were given was unravelling and cleaning old ships' tar-covered ropes and shredding the hemp into a reusable form, called oakum.

At Cold Baths Prison in Middlesex, 500 men sat in complete silence poring over their laborious task. Warders sat round the room on high stools, constantly scanning the men's faces to ensure that no one was talking. The air was thick with brown dust, which settled on their clothes and clogged their mouths, causing lung problems and sickness. In this eerie, unhealthy environment, each pair of hands picked up a two-foot length of old rope from a pile on the floor beside them and deftly untwisted the tarred strands. Apart from a hook used to grate the solid tar from the fibres, the work was done without the aid of tools and was extremely hard on the hands.

In another Middlesex prison, women also sat in dark, cold rooms picking oakum in strict silence for 12 hours. At the end of the day, the prisoners took their ball of hemp to be weighed and were expected to have picked at least 3 lbs.

Oakum was used in ship building for caulking or packing joints until iron and steel replaced wooden ships. It was also sold for making string or stuffing mattresses, hence the expression 'money for old rope'.

Ordeal

In some ancient societies, it was essential for a criminal to be tried and punished in order for his soul to pass to the afterlife. But if there were no witnesses to the crime, sometimes the only way to prove innocence or guilt was to leave the decision in the hands of the Almighty in a trial by ordeal.

In Saxon times, these were held frequently. For example, a pot of cow dung was mixed with oil, heated to boiling point and the accused was made to bury his arm in it. In the unlikely event that he wasn't burned, he was deemed to be innocent.

Another common method was making people walk barefoot over ploughshares, the metal blades of a plough, which had been heated in a fire. Trial by poison made the blindfolded prisoner retrieve a ring from a basket containing a poisonous snake, while in trial by fire, he had to walk through fire or carry a hot iron ball. The burns were bound and inspected three days later. Open sores denoted guilt and those who had healed were innocent. Many accused used bribery and corruption of the officiating clerics to ensure cool irons or coals which could be walked on safely.

These trials were attended by priests who sprinkled holy water and incanted prayers as though they were hoping the prisoner would escape harm, which, remarkably, did happen on numerous occasions.

It was once believed that the human body, under the influence of the gods, could withstand fire. This is confirmed by biblical stories such as Abraham escaping unscathed from the fiery furnace into which he had been hurled, and of Shadrach, Meshach and Abednego who emerged from a fiery furnace without a hair of their heads singed.

Emma, mother of Edward the Confessor and great-aunt of William the Conqueror, was subjected to this punishing test for being over friendly with the Bishop of Winchester. She was led, blindfolded, to the glowing hot irons and stepped swiftly ahead, crying out and asking when she would reach her moment of torment. When the blindfold was removed, she realised she had already crossed over, whereupon she dropped to her knees and thanked God for proving her innocence.

The cold water ordeal was used in England after the introduction of Christianity. The accused was stripped naked, bound hand and foot and thrown into water to see if he sank or not. Failure to sink was a sign of guilt. It was particularly popular during the witch hunts of the Middle Ages because it was believed that they were lighter than water and couldn't sink.

Ostracising

We use the expression being 'sent to Coventry' to mean being shunned by others, but what's the origin? One theory is that during the 17th century English Civil War, Coventry was a Puritan stronghold with a deep hatred of the military. The young women of the town were forbidden to speak to the soldiers and if they disobeyed, they were ostracised by the community as punishment.

Another explanation is that hostility to Puritans in other parts of the Midlands forced religious families from surrounding areas to move to Coventry where they could practise their religion freely.

There is yet another, more colourful, story that the name Coventry is derived from the covin tree, an oak, which stood in front of the castle in feudal times. The tree was used as the gallows, hence those to be executed were sent to the covin tree.

Many strict religious sects ostracise members who have broken their rules. This shunning ranges from temporary exclusion until the offender repents, or permanent banishment from the community. The psychological effects of ostracism can be devastating to the victim and their families, destroying marriages and separating children from their parents.

Outlawing

The life of an outlaw was glamorised forever by the stories of Robin Hood, robbing the rich to pay the poor. In reality, it was a hard and lonely life on the run, living in huts or caves, constantly in fear of being caught. An outlaw was someone who lived 'outside the law', making it one of the harshest penalties given. From Norman times, it was imposed on anyone who had defied the law by ignoring a summons to attend court or failing to plead in court after being charged with a crime. Anglo-Saxons also outlawed murderers who couldn't pay the blood money to the victim's family.

An outlaw became a public enemy to be

hunted to the death, but without any protection from the legal system. As far as society was concerned, he was a dead man, without any civil rights, and any child born to him couldn't inherit from him or from anyone else. No one was allowed to give food, shelter or other form of support, but they could kill him without fear of reprisal. Even if he joined a band and managed to lead a reasonably settled life, the danger of discovery and capture was ever present, and fighting, with its attendant wounds and sickness, a common event. If an outlaw was captured, he forfeited his right to trial and could be sent to the gallows immediately, regardless of his guilt or innocence.

When the Quakers were being persecuted in the 1600s, hundreds were outlawed for refusing to take an oath of allegiance to the Crown and all their possessions were seized.

The history of the American West wouldn't be complete without its cast of outlaws like Billy the Kid, Butch Cassidy and Jesse James. As recently as 1938, four Americans were sentenced to two years in jail for conspiring to harbour an outlaw.

PENDULUM

147

Pear

Aptly named the *poire d'angoisser* or pear of anguish, this awful torture was used throughout Europe. A small pear-shaped metal device, composed of four 'petals', was inserted into the prisoner's mouth, anus or vagina. The torturer then turned a screw which opened the petals, distending the cavity.

Pendulum

Devised by the inquisitors of Spain, and immortalised in Edgar Allan Poe's story *The Pit and the Pendulum*, this torture often drove victims mad before it completed its merciless scythe through the body. The victim was firmly secured to a table beneath a huge pendulum with a curved cutting edge hovering near the roof of the chamber. As it was set in motion, it swung to and fro, lengthening the shaft and bringing the deadly blade closer to the victim's face. First it slashed the skin, then continued until it had sliced right through the body unless the victim confessed in time.

Penance

With the exception of witchcraft and heresy, punishments handed out by the church authorities were generally more merciful than those administered under the criminal law of the State. The clergy were forbidden to inflict death or mutilation so they used discipline based on penitence which could nevertheless be devastating for the recipients. Being denied access to the Church or Communion was a terrible punishment because it meant the criminal was cast into eternal darkness and damnation. The sinner might be ordered to make a pilgrimage as his penance, to abstain from certain foods or exist on bread and water, sometimes for years.

King Edgar was told he must not wear his crown for seven years, while Henry II went on a pilgrimage of penitence to the tomb of Sir Thomas à Becket where he was severely scourged (whipped) by 80 bishops and monks.

Though the word of the Church was final, loopholes were found to ease the inconvenience of the sentence. The rich, for example, were allowed to perform their penances vicariously, paying one or more deputies to carry out the sentence on their behalf. This created a class of professional pilgrims willing to suffer for others – at a price.

It also created farcical situations like a wealthy man required to fast for 39 days sharing the time with others so he and 12 assistants had to live on bread and water for only three days each.

Picket

This punishment was used mainly by the cavalry and artillery. The victim stood on a stool and a piece of rope was tied around one wrist and attached to a post in the ground. He was hauled up by the wrist so his foot was just above the stool.

A second post with a pointed top was driven into the ground and his heel placed on the spike.

When the stool was removed, the victim had the intolerable choice of bearing his full weight on the spike or swinging by his wrist from the post. Though the sentence rarely lasted more than 15 minutes, it could cause lasting physical damage.

Pillory (also Stocks)

One of the traditional features of almost every village green in England was the stocks, a simple wooden construction once used to punish by shaming. The few remaining stocks today attract children and tourists who stick their feet through the holes and smile at a camera. It wasn't such a jolly jape for their predecessors who were sentenced to spend an hour or more sitting on the ground with their ankles clamped between the boards of the stocks.

If they were sentenced to the pillory, they stood, with their neck clamped and wrists secured. Then they were at the mercy of the crowds who, by their reaction, determined the degree of the punishment. Sex offenders were particularly hated. When Charles Hitchen was sentenced to an hour in the pillory for attempted sodomy, he was so terrified of the crowd's wrath, he donned a suit of armour. That didn't deter the angry mob from tearing it piece by piece from his body so he could feel the missiles they hurled.

In 1756, four condemned men were sentenced to an hour in the pillory before execution. The enraged mob hurled sticks, stones and other missiles with such ferocity, all four died before they could be hanged.

The author, Daniel Defoe, however, found guilty of satirising the government, spent a pleasant hour in the pillory being plied with food and drink. Either way, it was a cheap way to punish wrongdoers by letting the public carry out the sentence. Being 'pilloried' is an expression still used in our language to describe someone who is ridiculed, criticised or sneered at. The pillory and stocks were used to punish a wide range of offenders including bakers who sold bread which was short in weight and butchers who sold substandard meat.

Finger pillories or finger stocks were used to punish servants or children. As the name suggests, one finger, or all four, were trapped in the pillory so the offender couldn't walk away.

Drawings from Anglo-Saxon times show a primitive form of stocks was used then, and by the 14th century, they were in regular use. There was even a law which decreed that stocks should be set up in every town and village throughout England. 'Vagabonds, idle and suspect persons' were sentenced to three days and three nights, given only bread and water, and then kicked out of town. During the persecution of the Quakers in the 17th century, even young children were punished in the stocks for several hours.

One of the most notable occupants was Cardinal Wolsey in 1500 when he disgraced his office by over-imbibing at the Lymington village feast. A zealous Justice of the Peace for the Somerset area sent the churchman to the stocks to sober up.

Poison

Inviting a man to inflict punishment on himself by taking his own life would surely not work today. But in ancient Greece it was customary to make convicted Athenians drink a cup of hemlock or other poison as their death sentence. The philosopher Socrates was found guilty of opposing the gods and corrupting the youth in 399 BC. Despite offers from friends to help him escape, he refused to flee during his month-long incarceration, even though it would have been easy to have walked out of the prison. As the executioner prepared the infusion of hemlock, a poisonous herb related to carrots, devoted students and friends of the 70-year-old Socrates gathered to be with him in his final moments. He sent them away before he picked up the bowl and drank the deadly liquid, which caused a gradual and fatal paralysis.

In a modern day poisoning, Russian spy Alexander Litvinenko was apparently murdered with a radioactive substance hidden in a cup of tea. The former KGB officer fell ill after having the drink in London's Millennium Hotel in 2006 and died three weeks later. Police investigations revealed the presence of polonium 210 in Litvinenko's cup. The spy is believed to have been bumped off because he committed the ultimate betrayal of publicly criticising President Vladimir Putin.

Pressing

English Common Law used to stipulate that until a prisoner gave a plea, a trial couldn't be held so it was common for those arrested to be 'pressed to plea'.

This 'persuasion' was far less innocuous than words of encouragement, or even verbal threats. It meant literally pressing the accused's body with heavy weights until he either uttered a plea or his last breath.

The prisoner was laid on the ground, naked, and his arms and legs were drawn with cords fastened to several parts of the room. Increasingly heavy iron, stone or lead weights were piled on his chest.

Another reason prisoners were reluctant to plead was that if they begged for mercy and admitted guilt, they would be hanged which, in those days was a lingering and painful death. More importantly, as a convicted felon, all their possessions would be forfeited. If they stayed silent, they would die from being pressed, which wasn't much worse than being hanged, but they would die unconvicted, thereby saving their families from penury.

Major George Strangeways, a distinguished Civil War veteran, was subjected to pressing after refusing to plead to a murder charge in 1658. A wooden frame was placed on his body and iron weights piled on top. The pain was so excruciating, his friends hastened his death by standing on the frame.

A few years later, 80-year-old farmer Giles Corey was accused of witchcraft during the Salem witch trials in America. By refusing to plead, he elected to be pressed to death knowing his wealth would not be taken by the colony but be passed to his heirs. He became the only person in North American history to have been legally pressed to death.

When the torture was stopped occasionally to give Corey the chance to confess, all he whispered was 'More weight.' The ordeal lasted two days until he died from suffocation.

Celia Rygeway was accused of killing her husband and subjected to pressing in Nottingham jail because she refused to plead. After an incredible 40-day endurance, the woman was granted a pardon by Edward III as her survival was considered to be a miracle.

Otherwise known as *peine forte et dure* (strong and heavy pain), pressing was used for more than three hundred years. It wasn't until 1827 that our current law was passed assuming that no plea was the equivalent of a not guilty plea.

Prison

A jail sentence might seem preferable to some of the dreadful punishments inflicted on offenders, but in the mid-1700s, one in four prisoners died every year. They were herded together in cells without heating, bedding or sanitation, sometimes manacled together in irons weighing 18 kg. Vermin and disease were rife in these dank, subterranean hells. One cell in the Tower of London measured just over a metre square, making it impossible for the prisoner to sit or lie down.

If the walls of the Tower of London could speak, they would have volumes to tell about the dark deeds they've witnessed over the centuries. Occupants have included Lady Jane Grey and Sir Walter Raleigh. The last prisoner was Rudolf Hess, Hitler's deputy who flew to England in 1941 in a crazy bid to make peace. He was eventually imprisoned in Spandau, Berlin.

Most prisons were run privately, which meant that prisoners were overcrowded and exploited by money-grabbing jailers who charged them for everything. Many inmates couldn't leave jail at the end of their sentences because they couldn't afford to repay their debts.

One of the major causes of death was 'jail fever', an acute form of typhoid. It was so deadly that in 1577 more than 300 people who attended the assize held at Oxford Castle died in 40 hours, and in 1750, the germs from two infected convicts on trial at the Old Bailey ended up killing more than 50 people, including the entire jury, the Lord Mayor and two judges.

Prisons were originally places of detention, not punishment. There was little need for prisons since after their trial, felons were executed and those on lesser charges faced the stocks, pillory, whipping or a fine. Families of the condemned lived together in squalid jails until the execution day. Then the children would be wrenched tearfully from their mother's arms and put into the 'care' of the parish beadle. When old enough, they would be sent into household service as cheap domestic labour.

Many small jails were located at the rear of public houses and the publican acted as the jailer. The tiny cells were pitch dark because he covered up the panes to avoid paying window tax.

When a jury visited Newgate Prison to enquire about the death of a prisoner, they found such appalling conditions that the sheriff ordered the removal of the Quaker prisoners to nearby Bridewell Prison. The next afternoon, Londoners witnessed the remarkable sight of 32 prisoners walking two abreast, with their clothing bundles on their shoulders, through the streets of the city. When asked by passersby why they didn't escape as they were unguarded, they replied 'We have given our word.'

In Carlisle Castle during the 1745 rising, 300 captured Scotsmen were packed so tightly into an underground dungeon, the dead lay trampled beneath the bodies of the living. In an adjacent cell, the prisoners were manacled and chained by the neck. If they stepped too far onto a ledge in search of air, they hanged themselves.

One of the most notorious prisons was The Black Hole of Calcutta where 123 hapless inmates perished. During a hot and sultry Indian night in 1756, 146 prisoners were crammed into a cell measuring 6 metres square, with only two tiny windows to admit light and air. Many were trampled to death when the guards passed small quantities of water through the apertures and held up lights so they could watch the ensuing fights to reach the life-saving liquid. When the doors were opened the next morning, only 23 were left alive.

By the late 1700s, changes in social thinking led to a change in attitudes towards punishment. The horrible tortures and executions were gradually replaced with prison sentences as the notion of human rights took hold. Archaic prison conditions were improved and the idea of reforming and rehabilitating prisoners was developed, pioneered by John Howard, High Sheriff of Bedfordshire. His book *The State of Prisons*, published in 1774, illuminated the dreadful conditions in the country's jails.

It was in America where the first prisons, or penitentiaries (from penitent – sorry) were built aimed at reforming criminals by depriving them of their liberty. Of course, the idea didn't work, especially for hardened criminals, and today the United States is the world's leading jailer with more than two million behind bars.

Punishment Jacket

In the 1840s, prisoners were given near impossible tasks to complete during their incarceration and then punished for not doing them. If, for example, a man failed to complete the allotted number of turns he had to make on the crank (see **Crank)**, he would be put into the punishment jacket, which was similar to a straitjacket, with a rigid leather collar.

The prisoner was strapped to the wall in a standing position with his arms tied together across his chest. The collar was fastened so tightly around his neck there wasn't room for even a finger to be inserted. Victims were left in this position for up to a day, then sent back to complete their task, fed only bread and water which barely gave them the strength to live, let alone perform strenuous physical activities.

QUICKLIME

Quicklime

Nazi officers in occupied Poland didn't have enough bullets to kill all the Jews so they sought a way to dispense with them in large numbers. They did so by cramming them into railway carriages in which the floors were coated with quicklime, and leaving the train in a remote siding where no one could hear the screams. The victims took four or five days to die from excruciating burns. Thousands more Jews, men, women and children, were made to jump into pits lined with the deadly powder and then water was hosed on to them. This reacted with the quicklime and caused the pitiful victims to be boiled alive in an acid bath.

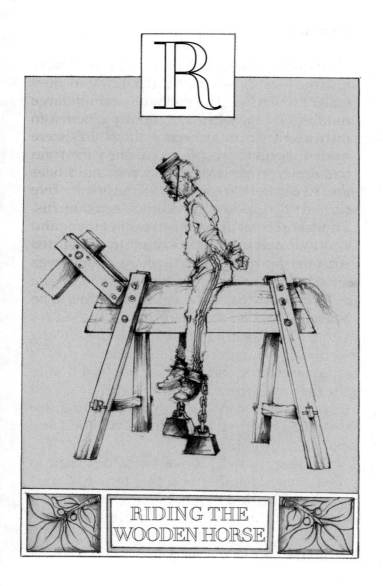

RIDING THE
WOODEN HORSE

Racking

Though English Common Law didn't recognise the legality of torture, that didn't mean it wasn't practised. The rack, for example, was used as long ago as the 13th century and was an instrument of torture throughout the 1600s as a means of extorting confessions. The victim was tied down on a board by the wrists and ankles and two rollers at each end of the board were turned in opposite directions, causing dislocation or total dismemberment of the limbs. An alternative method was to hang the prisoner up by the wrists on a pulley which stretched the body.

John Coustos, an Englishman living in Portugal in 1743 was arrested in Lisbon for being a member of the Freemasons. Refusing to divulge the secrets of his order, Coustos was sent to the torture chamber and tied to the rack with ropes bound so tightly, they cut into his flesh, causing profuse bleeding. He eventually fainted through loss of blood and excruciating pain.

Six weeks later, Coustos was returned to the torture chamber and this time his arms were tied behind him before the racking was carried out. His shoulders were dislocated and blood gushed from his mouth, but he still refused to speak.

He was racked on three separate occasions, the last time after having to have his shoulder bones reset before the torture could recommence. By then, his agony was too much to bear and he gave his inquisitors a list of Freemasons in Lisbon and details of their practices. However, he steadfastly refused to become a Catholic to gain his release and was kept in prison for another year.

Guy Fawkes was put on the rack in 1605 in an attempt to obtain the names of his fellow gunpowder plotters. He was injured so severely, he had to be carried to the scaffold for his execution.

Riding the Wooden Horse

The military, it seems, were impressively inventive when it came to devising punishments for their men. Though imposed for relatively minor offences, such as drinking or rioting, the wooden horse was nonetheless extremely painful and, on occasions, fatal.

A board with a narrow, or even sharpened, edge was mounted on four legs to which a rudely-fashioned head and tail were attached. The soldier being punished was set astride the 'horse' with his hands tied behind his back and heavy weights tied to each foot.

Garret Segersen, a Dutch soldier in the American army, was made to ride the wooden horse for three days with a 50 lb weight on each foot, for the crime of stealing chickens.

Connecticut horse thief James Brown was sentenced to 15 lashes and an hour riding the wooden horse for each week of his eight-week jail sentence.

The wooden horse was eventually abandoned in the English army because of the permanent injury it caused to the user.

Running the Gauntlet

We still use the expression 'running the gauntlet' to mean facing an ordeal or challenge, but this has nothing to do with wearing stout gloves.

The word is actually a corruption of a Swedish word *antlope*, which is the passage between two files of soldiers. It was a common military punishment in 17th century England and on the Continent. The entire regiment was assembled and stood six men deep. They were split so three rows of soldiers faced inwards on either side and each man was given a lash. The culprit, stripped naked to the waist, had to run or walk through the two groups of soldiers, often preceded by a sergeant who held a sword against the man's chest to prevent him from passing too quickly. The soldiers were instructed to strike with force, blows which often proved fatal. If the man survived, he might be reinstated in his post, his slate considered to have been wiped clean. Some were sent back for a second, and likely the last, run of the gauntlet.

Either way, this was considered a more honourable method of punishment than beating or being pilloried since the soldier could take his punishment like a man, upright among his comrades.

In a New World version of the punishment, a parson named Oldham, after being thrown into a Plymouth, Mass. jail for his bad behaviour, was ordered to pass through a guard of musketeers who were instructed to 'give him a thump on ye breech with ye end of his musket, then they bid him goe and mende his manners.'

Perhaps the nearest modern equivalents to running the gauntlet are the traditional university initiation rituals. These physical or mental ordeals, known as hazing in North America and ragging or fagging in Britain, tend to straddle the line between abuse and harmless rites of passage. A favourite 'punishment' is to make the initiate crawl through a line of students who each inflict a swift stroke on the retreating backside using a flat, wooden paddle.

SCOLD'S
BRIDLE

Scalping

Though we tend to associate scalping with Native Americans in the Wild West, the practice actually dates back 2,500 years to Scythian warriors of central Asia.

After they'd killed enemy warriors, they used a metal tool to make a horizontal incision across the back of the skull and then peeled back the skin.

Scalping was practised in many parts of Europe during the early centuries of civilisation, in the belief that the owner's powers were transferred to the scalper. The scalps of brave or powerful warriors were held in high esteem because of this.

North American Indians scalped by grasping the hair on the crown of the head with the left hand and passing a knife around it and under the skin, tearing off a piece of skin and hair about the size of the palm of the hand.

Scalping in the pioneer days of America was by no means confined to the Indians.

White pioneers collected Indian scalps for the bounties offered by Governor Kieft in 1641. The idea caught on with successive governors, so for the next 150 years it was open season for scalping as the French, who sided with the Indians, offered bounties for British scalps and the British offered bounties for French scalps.

Scavenger's Daughter

During the reign of Henry VIII, Sir Leonard Skeffington, Lieutenant of the Tower of London, invented a torture device which, unlike the rack, was easily portable to anywhere in the country. This made it ideal for torturers to take on their travels in search of treason and heresy. The victim was made to kneel in a hinged iron hoop which was locked and tightened, compressing the body horribly. The pain it induced was usually effective in securing a confession.

Scold's Bridle (or Brank)

For more than two hundred years, women were punished for being troublesome or disruptive by having to wear a gagging device within a metal cage worn on the head. The metal 'tongue' which went into the mouth to stop them from speaking was usually smooth, but sometimes it was deliberately spiked or roughened to cause greater pain. Originally used in Scotland, the bridle became an alternative punishment to the ducking-stool.

In some 17th century timbered houses, a hook was fixed on one side of the open fireplace so if the wife misbehaved, the husband would send for the local jailer to bring the bridle. 'If you don't rest your tongue, I'll send for the bridle and hook you up,' they threatened. Sometimes a woman was bridled and led through the streets to be jeered at by the crowd or chained to the pillory, whipping-post or market cross.

Oddly, though many men would qualify for being quarrelsome or a public nuisance, they generally escaped the bridle. One exception was James Brodie, a blind beggar in prison for murder in Nottingham, who made so much noise in prison awaiting his execution that a brank was used to silence him.

Shaming

Our predecessors could get away with almost any kind of punishment without do-gooders or human rights activists intervening. Compared with some of the barbaric practices they used, shaming seems extremely mild, though modern lawmakers may disagree.

The ancient custom of holding a man up to ridicule and public condemnation if he had beaten his wife or been unfaithful was called 'riding the stang'. An effigy of the offender,

172

wearing a card with the offence written on it, was mounted on a long pole or ladder. A makeshift band playing tin cans and whistles with buckets for drums was led by a speech-maker who bellowed a bawdy verse about the incident as the effigy was carried through the village. For three nights the noisy parade publicised the miscreant's behaviour, leaving no one in doubt as to who he was and what he'd done. On the third night, the effigy was burnt. A variation of this practice in the south of England was called 'skimmington riding' in which a cart or donkey carried two people, one representing the husband and the other, the wife, who beat each other using a skimmer and a ladle.

These harmless but effective chastisements were commonly practised until nearly the end of the 19th century.

In literature, the classic example of a shamed or 'scarlet' women is adulteress Hester Prynne in the novel *The Scarlet Letter*, by Nathaniel Hawthorne. She is made to wear the letter A around her neck to proclaim her sin, a sentence which caused her profound shame and mental anguish.

Similarly, in 1780, Sarah Lund was ordered to stand on the market cross in Wakefield, Yorkshire, for an hour on market day holding a sign saying 'Common scold' (nag).

Shaming traders who tried to cheat their poverty-stricken customers gave the public an opportunity to vent their anger against them. The baker who gave short weight with his loaves was paraded through the town with bread tied round his neck. The fishmonger who sold stale fish to the poor was punished by having to wear a collar of the smelly fish round his shoulders while his customers hurled abuse. A heretic who was also a strict Jew, was sent to prison and ordered to be fed solely on pork, a banned food under Jewish law.

Sometimes a drunk was made to walk through the town encased in a beer barrel with holes cut in the top and sides for his head and hands to protrude. A sign proclaiming 'I am wearing this for getting drunk' completed the public humiliation. The 'drunkard's cloak' or 'barrel shirt' was equally effectively for thieves.

More recently, The Public Health (London) Act of 1936 allowed a sign giving details of the offence to be posted for 21 days on premises which had sold bad food.

It was a sure-fire way to lose customers.

When Texas judges tried similar shaming tactics, there was huge opposition because the effect of the punishment extends beyond the shaming. The offender becomes a victim of harassment, violence and eviction by hostile people, and can be driven to suicide by their abusive treatment.

Nevertheless, Judge Ted Poe has recently handed out hundreds of sentences requiring offenders to advertise their crime: a drunk driver had to stand in front of a bar with the sign: 'I killed two people while driving drunk'. And Judge J. Manuel Banales made 15 sex offenders put signs in their front gardens reading: 'Danger, Registered Sex Offender Lives Here'.

In Ohio, two men were given the option of 60 days in jail or walking down Main Street in women's clothing after throwing beer bottles at a woman's car. They chose the latter. In the same state, a defendant found guilty of sending false fire alarms was sentenced to go to each fire department in the court's district of Painesville and make a public apology.

Sleep Deprivation

One of the simplest and most effective methods used by the witch-hunters of the 17th century to extract confessions was depriving victims of their sleep. John Lowes, an elderly parson, was marched around his cell for three days and nights without rest until he confessed.

One old widow, Elizabeth Clarke, was made to sit on a stool so high, her feet didn't touch the ground. She was forced to stay awake for several days until she admitted being a witch and named 31 accomplices.

In the House of Commons on 1 July 1830, during the course of a speech on slavery in the colonies, a case was cited of an English gentlewoman who, suspecting her slave to have stolen from her, imprisoned the young negress in the stocks for 17 days, during which period she was deprived of sleep by having red pepper rubbed into her eyes.

In America, the founding fathers dreamed up original ways of inflicting punishment. One was a head cage made of iron strips curved into a tulip shape. The victim had to endure bearing its heavy weight during the day but worse, the endless succession of sleepless nights because it was impossible to relax the head.

Sleep deprivation was also a commonly-used torture for political prisoners, aimed at breaking down their mental resistance to propaganda.

Squassation

Also known as the torture of the pulley,

strappado or reverse hanging, this was the first torture of the Inquisition. The victim was stripped and shackled, and the wrists tied behind the back. A stout rope was fastened to the wrists and carried over a pulley fixed to the roof of the torture chamber. Iron weights, around 100 pounds, were attached to the irons on the prisoner's feet. If he still refused to confess, he was given a severe whipping and the ropes were pulled, raising the victim towards the ceiling. Then the rope was slackened and abruptly stopped, wrenching every bone, joint and nerve in the body.

This torture was used by the Nazis and it has reportedly been used in Iraq, Iran and Turkey. In November 2003, a man died during an interrogation session at Abu Ghraib prison in Iraq after being subjected to squassation. The US military ruled the death a homicide.

Stoning

'Stone him to death, because he tried to turn you away from the Lord your God, who brought you out of Egypt out of the land of slavery.' Deuteronomy. 13.9

Stoning, or lapidation, is one of the oldest methods of punishment. St Stephen became the first Christian martyr when he was stoned to death in AD 36 for blasphemy against Moses and God.

During this slow execution the victim suffers prolonged pain, dehydration and heat exhaustion, as well as massive head injuries. Those condemned to death are often buried waist or neck deep in sand with their heads covered by sheets. Women are buried deeper than men to cover their breasts. The missile throwers are often members of the victim's family or community and they are banned under the Islamic code from using stones so large that only one or two would be fatal. The smaller the stones, the longer the suffering of the victim.

Despite the fact that stoning isn't mentioned in the Koran, it's still a legal sentence in some Islamic countries governed by Sharia law particularly for the crimes of prostitution, adultery and murder.

T

TARRING &
FEATHERING

Tarring and Feathering

The practice of tarring and feathering goes back to the days of the crusades and has been used as both a punishment and as mob vengeance. Richard the Lionheart decreed that any robber found among the crusaders should have his head shaven, then boiling pitch poured on it and covered with feathers.

The punishment wasn't used much after that until it was revived by the American colonists who used it against British officials in the 1700s. Tar was readily available in the shipyards and everyone used feathers in their pillows, so it was a convenient and effective discipline, seldom fatal but extremely uncomfortable.

The victim would be stripped, partially or completely, before being covered in hot tar. As this requires a fairly high temperature to melt (approx. 60° C), it would have caused painful blistering on the skin. Then the person was rolled around in a pile of chicken, or other fowl, feathers which readily stuck to the tar. Often the victim was paraded through the town on a cart as further humiliation.

The punishment has been used periodically throughout history and in various countries though it was largely an American practice. In addition to the early settlers who used it to show their disapproval of new taxes, African Americans were punished with tarring and feathering for often specious crimes.

German collaborators were given the treatment in France after World War II, especially those women accused of fraternising with enemy soldiers.

Likewise, there were many incidents of tarring and feathering during the Northern Ireland Troubles, many of the victims being women who had had sexual relationships with British soldiers. When victims were taken to hospital, nurses had to check for fractures before they set about the tricky job of removing the tar or, more likely, diesel oil. Eucalyptus worked best and the Royal Victoria Hospital in Belfast used more of it than anywhere else in the United Kingdom.

The latest incident occurred in August 2007, when a Belfast drug dealer was tarred, feathered and tied to a lamp-post.

Tawse

The tawse, or the belt, was the most common punishment inflicted in Scottish schools until corporal punishment was banned in 1998. The 1968 Code of Practice restricted its use on the hands, but prior to that, naughty boys were beaten on their legs and backsides.

The word is the plural of 'taw', a Scottish word meaning a thong of a whip. It was made from a thick, hard piece of leather, with the ends split into two or three tails.

Several schools in Aberdeenshire boasted 'cooling stanes', large stones just outside the school door to which pupils who had just been belted could rush at play times to sit on and take some of the stinging from their wounds.

According to a former pupil at St Andrew's RC School in Dumfries, the tawse was used daily for trivial offences. More serious ones were punished in front of the assembled school when boys were brutally beaten on the bare backside by the headmaster, while two male teachers held down the struggling victim.

Thumbscrews

These simple little devices were handy to carry around and extremely effective in causing sufficient pain to get confessions. The victim's finger or thumb was inserted into a split ring which was tightened with a screw. Some had studs inside them to increase the suffering. Few who were subjected to this torture failed to confess, it was so painful. In extreme use, it crushed the finger to a mass of pulp. In Scotland, it was called a thumbkins and was used until the end of the 17th century.

Tickling

Those of us who are ticklish know that at first it makes you laugh, but prolonged tickling becomes unendurable.

In a punishment known as goat's tongue or tickling torture, the ancient Romans covered the victim's feet with salt or a sweet substance and let a goat lick it off.

The initial sensation was a pleasant tickle, but it became increasingly painful as the soles of the feet were blistered and licked raw by the goat's rough tongue.

Prince Vlad of Transylvania enjoyed using this torture on Turkish prisoners who had a constant stream of salt water dripped onto their feet from above.

Tickling as punishment was also used when people were confined in the stocks, their exposed feet being an open invitation for tormentors.

The Chinese tickle torture was supposedly used on the nobility because it left no marks on the victim. The method is reported to have been used in the courts of the Han Dynasty, though some historians dispute this claim.

Transportation

Shipping the worst convicts from England to America was hailed as a brilliant idea in the late 1500s. The vast expanses of the New World had just been discovered by Christopher Columbus and getting rid of troublesome criminals not only safeguarded our society but also saved on the cost of building prisons.

Transportation was often imposed as an alternative to capital punishment and the sentence was seven years, fourteen years or for life. Even so, English judges handed out unreasonably long and savage sentences for trivial offences such as 18-year-old Edward Baker who was given life because he stole a pocket handkerchief.

In 1830, farm labourers in Salisbury, Wiltshire, were struggling to raise families in grinding poverty amid the threat of unemployment with the introduction of machinery. Their desperation led to some rioting, which was quickly quelled, but the consequences were dreadful. Thirty-four were sentenced to death and others transported for life. Their womenfolk and children wept bitterly as the men, who had committed no crime other than trying to feed their families, were taken away, never to be seen again.

Though it was an offence for a convict to return from transportation, many men risked death so they could see their loved ones once more. If they were caught twice, they were hanged.

Women convicts fared no better than men. Heavily chained, they were herded like cattle into the bowels of the ship to face whatever fate lay in store for them. The Quaker Elizabeth Fry visited every convict ship that left the Thames, distributing knitting and patchwork to keep the women occupied during the arduous voyage.

Initially, a 'hundred dissolute persons' were sent to Virginia, followed by many more Quakers transported during the reign of Charles II.

The majority of those sent died either *en route* during the four to six-month journey, or under the rigours of slavery on the plantations within America or the West Indies.

The convicts who survived were actually better off in their new lives than they would have been back home. The law-abiding settlers of Virginia, though, weren't too happy about having criminals in their communities, especially as some of them showed little inclination to work hard, but the British government refused to halt the practice. The problem was resolved when transportation ceased during the American War of Independence, after which plantation owners starting using a cheaper source of labour in slaves shipped from Africa.

In 1786, the British established a penal colony at Botany Bay, in the newly-discovered continent of Australia. The first voyage carrying 736 convicts, male and female, took 252 days and claimed the lives of 48 passengers in the sweltering heat of the airless hold. They arrived in the middle of the Australian summer and bleakly surveyed the barren scrubland where they were meant to cultivate their food. Most of them had come from the streets of London and few had ever seen a farm, let alone worked on one. The English farming methods and crops were totally unsuited to the subtropical climate, and famine dogged their days.

If that seemed a bad lot, it was nothing compared to the life endured by the dangerous convicts sent to Norfolk Island, 1,000 miles east of Australia. Known as the 'Island of the Damned', it was governed by three successive bullies who outdid each other in the brutality of their treatments. The second of these, Major Joseph Foveaux, lashed one prisoner so frequently, the man's collar bones were stripped of flesh and protruded like sticks of ivory .

Foveaux was followed by Lieutenant-Colonel James Morriset who had men lashed week after week until the lacerated flesh on their backs and buttocks became infected. Their only hope was that maggots would invade the open wounds and eat the infected tissue.

The French transported their convicts to a remote island in the South Caribbean Sea. It was dubbed 'Devil's Island' and life there was diabolical in every way. Prisoners were confined in a wooden stockade on the edge of dense jungle and shark-infested seas, both of which made escape near impossible.

The island's most renowned resident was Rene Belbenoit whose audacious bids for freedom earned him celebrity status. He attempted to flee several times in primitive rafts and canoes but was caught and kept in solitary confinement for months in a disease-ridden pit. At last, in 1935, Belbenoit and some fellow prisoners landed in British-held Trinidad after two weeks afloat in a dugout canoe they'd made.

Treadmill

The treadmill was introduced into prisons in 1818 as part punishment, part hard labour but originally intended to keep criminals usefully employed.

It looked like a giant 20 ft paddle wheel with 24 stepping boards around a six foot cylinder. Prisoners lined up side by side and held on to a handrail as they trod on the endless steps like hamsters in a cage, turning the internal cylinder in a continuous motion.

Men would have to use the treadmill eight or more hours a day, in 15-minute shifts, in order to provide mechanical power for a grist mill, fan or a water pump. They were required to climb the equivalent of between 5,000 and 14,000 vertical feet every day, an average of twice the height of Ben Nevis. It was not only hard work and very boring, it also took its toll on the weaker inmates.

U

UNUSUAL
SENTENCES

189

Unusual Sentences

Today, most 'lifers' are freed within a few years, in stark contrast to the past, when a life sentence in jail meant just that. In 1690, John Bernardi was arrested for a political offence and thrown into Newgate jail. He wrote that he was 'loaded with irons and put into a dark and stinking apartment.' Bernardi was kept in prison for nearly 50 years without being brought to trial and he died in 1736. He did manage to acquire a wife who bore him ten children within the confines of his cell.

In 2002, Birmingham double killer, Andrew Aston, earned the dubious honour of receiving an unprecedented 26 life sentences. Only 22 other prisoners out of a prison population of 69,000 at that time had tariffs for the rest of their natural lives. The judge told Aston that, although he could be considered for parole in 14 years, he was making a recommendation to the Home Secretary that Aston serve 'substantially longer'.

A Swiss tourist was sentenced to 10 years in jail by a court in Thailand in 2007 for the unusual crime of *lèse-majesté* or insulting the monarch. Oliver Jufer, 57, took a tipple too many during a trip to Chiang Mai and was caught on a surveillance camera spraying black paint on posters of King Bhumibol Adulyadej.

He pleaded guilty to five charges of insulting the king and defacing public property, but was later pardoned by the Monarch and deported.

Unusual Prisoners

Perhaps the most unusual, but most popular, prisoners in history were the 237 female convicts aboard a floating brothel bound for Botany Bay. They left Plymouth in 1789 on the *Lady Julian* and during the year-long passage, were obliged to service the crew. Whenever they docked, sailors from other ships, as well as locals who had heard the rumour, rowed out to the *Lady Julian* for a swift assignation with the women.

By the time they reached Australia, some of the on-board relationships had blossomed into love and 12 babies had been born. Most of the unions were doomed, however, when the women were sold on arrival or sent off to remote islands to complete their sentence.

The riddle of a nameless Frenchman in a mask, who spent 34 years in prison, has never really been solved. Novelist Alexandre Dumas gave his version of the story in his 1848 novel *The Man in the Iron Mask*, suggesting the prisoner was the elder twin of King Louis XIV, imprisoned to prevent him from claiming the throne. Another idea was that the prisoner was actually Louis who had been locked away by an illegitimate brother who had taken on his identity.

A more widely accepted hypothesis is that the man was Louis's natural father. His mother gave birth to the boy after 22 barren years of marriage and 14 years after she and her impotent husband, Louis XIII, had separated, leaving no doubt that he wasn't the father. The biological father, who had been carefully selected for his role of fathering the next king, was sent away immediately the baby was conceived. He returned to France 31 years later where, seeing his resemblance to Louis XIV, the king's agents kidnapped and imprisoned him.

From then on, until his death of natural causes in 1703, the man was hidden behind a black mask, believed to be velvet, rather than iron. He ate and slept in the mask, watched constantly by two musketeers who were ready to kill him if he removed it.

The mystery man wasn't murdered because Louis XIV didn't want to commit patricide.

Another unusual prisoner was Robert F. Stroud, who was jailed for a brutal murder in

1909 and ended up a legend, the erroneously dubbed Birdman of Alcatraz. Stroud was sent to prison in Washington State where he assaulted a member of staff and stabbed a fellow inmate. His sentence was increased and he was transferred to Leavenworth Jail in Kansas where he spent 30 years. During this time he raised 300 canaries in his cells and wrote two authoritative books on them.

Prone to violent outbursts, he stabbed a guard to death in front of 1,100 inmates in the prison mess hall and was given the death sentence, which was commuted to life.

But when the prison authorities discovered the equipment he was using to make products to sell for bird ailments was actually being used to construct a still for brewing alcohol, Stroud was transferred to the infamous Alcatraz Prison, the toughest in the country, located on a rocky outcrop in San Francisco Bay.

Here he ended his days in isolation, but became known as the Birdman of Alcatraz, memorably, if inaccurately, portrayed by Burt Lancaster in the Hollywood movie.

Firstly, Stroud was definitely not the mild-mannered ornithologist the actor made him out to be, and secondly, Stroud was never allowed to keep birds in Alcatraz.

Another of the prison's most famous inmates was the American gangster, Al Capone. Despite his gangland crimes, he was only convicted of tax evasion and sentenced to 11 years in jail. He spent five years in Alcatraz during which time his mental stability deteriorated due to syphilis, a disease which killed him in 1947.

When an imposing American woman named Elizabeth Carmichael designed a three-wheeled car which could do seventy miles to the gallon, Americans applauded. After all, it was 1974, and the price of petrol had quadrupled. Still, their gas-guzzling vehicles had to be filled. Carmichael toured the country promoting her invention, called the Dale, and to raise $6 million for her car company.

Unfortunately, when the vehicle was investigated, it turned out to be more Heath Robinson than Henry Ford, put together with scrap parts and bent coat hangers, and powered by a lawnmower engine.

The fabrication didn't end there. Far from being the mother of five, as claimed, she was, in fact their father, Jerry Dean Michael. After his 1975 trial, Michael disappeared for nine years and was found living in the town of Dale, Texas, as a woman, claiming to have undergone sex-change surgery. Medical examination disproved this and Michael was sent to an all-male prison to serve his sentence.

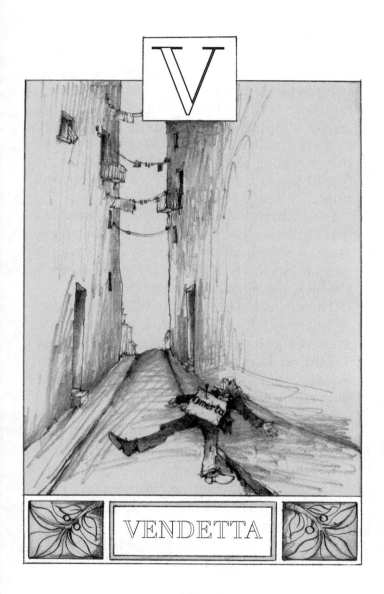

VENDETTA

Vendetta

In societies where family ties are strong, vengeance is assured. But feuds between families can last through generations and cause a ripple effect of pain and misery. Perhaps the most poignant was that between the Capulet and Montague families in Shakespeare's tragic story of Romeo and Juliet.

In Southern Italy, home of the vendetta, one real life blood feud which cost 35 lives over 30 years, was brought to an end by a 25-year-old woman, so worn down by grief and despair, she blew the whistle on the perpetrators.

The dispute started in the 1970s with a case of horse-rustling and a disagreement over grazing rights between the Ciaravella and the Tarantino families. That started the traditional pattern of revenge by the male next-of-kin to protect the family's *omerta* or honour.

The worst incident came in 1981 when an entire family of five were slaughtered in their home. Their bodies, it's believed, were ground to a paste and fed to the pigs.

Of the eight Tarantino brothers, six have died violently in payment of the blood-price for the deaths.

As a result of the information given to the police by the young housewife and partner of a ringleader, 90 gangsters were rounded up. However, in a country where the rule of vendetta is that it never ends until everyone is dead, no one believes the story's over.

The most notorious organised crime organisation in the world is the Mafia in which each gang is known as a 'family', whether or not they're related. Their bloody vendettas were graphically portrayed in *The Godfather* novel and movie.

Italy isn't alone in having a long history of vendettas. They flourish wherever families are strong and the rule of law is weak. In Arab countries, the ancient code of 'an eye for an eye' prevails over any judicial system and is fuelled by the clash of competing faiths.

Gangland vendettas which smear the streets of our cities with blood, are these days more likely to be spawned by drug deals and protection rackets than interfamilial disputes.

During the 1950s and 60s, gangsters, the Kray Brothers and their rivals, the Richardsons, ruled the East London underworld under the watchful eye of their devoted mothers.

Even in a country like Israel, which is torn by intense political strife, underworld vendettas are rife. Six main gangs or families battle over control of lucrative illegal businesses.

'Crime is literally a family business for Israeli mobsters,' says Professor Robert Rockaway, Jewish History Professor at Tel Aviv University, 'and blood runs thicker than water.'

Vigilantes

He was a drug-dealing gang boss, who pedalled his wares to neighbourhood children. They were men prepared to take the law into their own hands to rid the streets of gangland violence. As the police stood helplessly by, the vigilantes doused their target with petrol and set him alight. Then they pumped bullets into his smouldering body.

This was Cape Town, South Africa, in the 1990s, one example of vigilante action to mete out punishment where the authorities have failed to act.

The word *vigilante* is Spanish, meaning private security agent, and probably came into the English language from America.

Before law and order was established in the Wild West, pioneers formed committees to try and enforce it. Cattle rustlers would be found with a rope round their necks; trouble makers horsewhipped or run out of town. In extreme cases, the culprits were lynched.

Vigilantes were particularly active during the great Californian Gold Rush when the crime rate was inevitably high, especially along San Francisco's lawless Barbary Coast.

Today, vigilantes operate throughout the world in a range of guises, dispensing their own, often violent, form of justice on victims. When child killer Ian Huntley's ex-girlfriend, Maxine Carr, was released from prison, vigilantes threatened she'd be dead in six days for protecting him.

The Sombra Negra or Black Shadow, a group of mainly retired police officers and military personnel in El Salvador, are committed to cleansing the country of 'impure' social elements.

Perhaps the most feared of all vigilantes were the Tonton Macoutes, the brutal personal police force of Haitian dictator Francois Duvalier (Papa Doc). These thugs were given free rein to torture, kill and extort, rooting out and murdering hundreds of Duvalier's opponents. Little changed when he died in 1971 and was succeeded by his son, Jean-Claude Duvalier (Baby Doc).

From Desperate Dan to Spiderman, super heroes pledged to right wrongs have inspired readers of all ages. The fact that they operated outside the law added an extra frisson. Hollywood, too, loves to portray vigilantes as modern day Robin Hoods and movies on the theme include *Dirty Harry, Taxi Driver* and *V for Vendetta*.

Vilification

If you call someone a 'poofter' or 'slut' in parts of Australia, you could find yourself in court on a charge of vilification. Meaning simply 'slander' or 'defamation', the offence is designed to stamp out racism and religious intolerance.

After the war in Iraq was launched, the Queensland Anti-Discrimination Commission distributed information pamphlets in several languages warning people of the penalties of breaking the vilfication law.

Vivisection

Though we tend to associate vivisection with animal experimentation, there have been cases involving human dissection. After the Second World War, thirty Japanese Army officers and medics were charged with conducting surgical experiments on eight American pilots at the Kyushu University medical facility. They tried to see if they could remove and replace the brain or put stitches into human hearts. All the patients died.

In a separate incident, Akira Makino, a medical auxiliary in the Imperial Navy, admitted he cut open ten Filipino prisoners, including two teenage girls. He amputated their limbs and cut out their internal organs while they were still alive. Mr Makino said he was forced to perform vivisections or be killed.

WHEEL

Walking the Plank

This is one form of punishment which appears to have its foundation in myth rather than reality.

Its most famous reference was in the novel *Peter Pan* when people were made to walk the plank and, of course, in subsequent film versions of the story. The addition of shark-infested waters added to the drama of the 'punishment'.

However, there is little or no evidence that sailors were ever actually made to walk along a wooden plank from the side of the ship and until they fell off the end into the water to drown. It's more likely they were simply tossed straight into the sea by their shipmates.

Washing the Mouth Out

It was often believed that the soul of a heretic or witch was corrupt and evil. Before they faced their punishment, the condemned were cleansed by being forced to drink scalding water or to eat hot coals or soap. Our modern day threat of making cheeky children wash out their mouths with soapy water has derived from this ancient practice.

Water Torture

Water has always been used as a bloodless but effective form of torture or punishment, often causing unendurable torment for the victim. A 16th century lawyer discovered that water falling a drop at a time on the human forehead could drive the victim frantic.

Dropping water continuously onto a sensitive part of the body can even be fatal, and can extract a confession from the toughest criminal in minutes. In New York State Prison in 1858, a healthy man named Simon Moore was kept in a shower bath for nearly an hour and died immediately he was taken out.

In ancient Rome, victims were confined in a hot-air bathroom where the steamy heat caused slow suffocation.

One of the most widely-used methods of torture during the Inquisition was slow drowning. Water was poured into the victim's mouth until his stomach swelled to bursting point, which caused head pain and ultimate asphyxiation. Sometimes a cloth was put over the victim's mouth before the water was poured in. As the material became saturated, it sank into his throat, choking him.

A version of this torture, called *chiffon*, is still used in Algeria. A rag is stuffed into the victim's mouth and dirty water, bleach, urine or chemicals are poured through it until the stomach is distended. Then the torturers stamp on it to force the victim to vomit, before the torture is repeated.

Water boarding – pouring water over the face of a pinioned victim until he gags – came to public notice in recent years as a torture being used on detainees in the US-run Guantanamo Bay camp in Cuba.

Victims dunked into very cold water can suffer from hypothermia and there have been reports that the Chinese use a water dungeon to punish dissidents. They are immersed neck-deep in a pool of filthy water and left for up to weeks at a time which causes skin sores and muscle paralysis.

Wheel

This was a popular form of capital punishment in France and Germany during the Middle Ages. In one form of it, the victim was bound to a cart wheel, or to a broad wheel resembling a cylinder, which was rolled down a hill over iron spikes fixed in the ground. A variation was to drive a heavy wagon repeatedly over the body until the bones were broken.

In 1761, 86-year-old John Calas of Toulouse, who was accused of strangling his son, was sentenced to be tortured to make him reveal the name of his accomplices.

Then he was 'broken alive on the wheel, to receive the last stroke after he had lain two hours, and then to be burnt to ashes.' The executioner wielded an iron bar and set about shattering every limb and bone. Often, an executioner could accomplish this without even piercing the skin. The wheel would be propped up so onlookers could hear the dying agonies of the victim.

Whirligig

Petty crimes were often punished in the Army by putting soldiers into a cage which was made to revolve at great speed, causing nausea and pain. There are reports from the American army that with excessive use, the treatment led to insanity and mental damage.

Witches

Until the 15th century, witchcraft was accepted by the church as being a relatively harmless pursuit, but in 1484, Pope Innocent

VIII changed his mind. He told the inquisitors to set on witches like a pack of hungry wolves as these cavorters with the devil had to be rooted out and exterminated. Horrible tortures were inflicted on the suspects in an attempt to extract an admission of guilt.

Several different methods were used to 'prove' someone was a witch such as looking for a 'diabolical mark', a mole or birthmark on the body, which proved association with the devil. In the belief that these marks would fail to bleed if punctured, women were prodded all over their bodies with a long, thin needle to discover a spot that didn't yield blood. It was an intensely painful experience which often resulted in a 'confession'.

A thumb might be tied to a toe and the accused thrown into a pond to see if he or she floated. Drowning proved innocence but floating indicated guilt because the body rejected the baptismal water.

It was believed that witches possessed a demon in animal form so the accused were left in a vermin-infested cell until a rat or mouse inevitably ran by, thus proving the presence of the demon.

Any natural disaster which occurred in the area, such as a failed harvest, was attributed to the work of witches. Communities lived in fear and mistrust, knowing that if individuals or families were affected, they would rush to denounce their neighbour. Even children denounced their parents and saw them hanged.

Witch-finding could be a lucrative business. One of the most prolific was Matthew Hopkins who toured East Anglia in the 1600s routing witches with feverish zeal and the lure of a fat purse from the town's coffers. He was given 20 shillings for every witch put to death, which was a tidy sum in those days. Claiming to have a list from the devil of all the witches in England, he stooped to any level to net his catch. One trick was to jab the victim with a spring-loaded knife. The blade retracted, leaving no mark on the skin, which was clear proof of sorcery to all who witnessed the test. Hopkins duped everyone for 14 months, during which time he sent 400 people to the hangman.

During America's infamous Salem witch trials in 1692, 19 women were led to the gallows and died with pious dignity. The last words of Sarah Good were to a corpulent inquisitor, denying the accusation of witchcraft. 'You are a liar,' she cried. 'I am no more a witch than you are a wizard, and if you take away my life, God will give you blood to drink.' Tradition claims that her prophecy was fulfilled and the man died a few years later from an internal haemorrhage. Tragically, the community later regretted denouncing each other and this was the last witchcraft trial held in America.

There are no definitive figures for the total number of witches executed during roughly 250 years of persecution but historians generally agree on around 40,000.

X SHAPED
CROSS

Xerxes

As the Persian Army marched on Greece around 480 BC, storm-whipped waves smashed a strategic bridge in front of them, halting their progress. Their angry leader, King Xerxes, decided to punish the waters that had destroyed the bridge and ordered his men to give the strait 300 lashes and a verbal chastisement.

Camp X-Ray

Detainees in Cuba's notorious Camp X-Ray were thrown into wire cages with concrete floors where they were shackled for up to 15 hours at a time, claims a freed British captive. Jamal al-Harith, who was held for two years, said prisoners were put in hand and leg irons which cut into their skin, and frequently assaulted with fists, feet and batons.

As part of the ongoing psychological torment, detainees were deprived of sleep, forced to kneel for hours and naked vice girls were sent in to degrade devout Muslims. Poor food and medical treatment left the men sick and malnourished. Jamal said he knew of 11 detainees who had had legs amputated and was told the Americans had removed more tissue than was necessary.

A website designer from Manchester, Jamal was arrested after straying into Afghanistan during a trip to Pakistan.

Camp X-Ray has been replaced by Camp Delta in another part of Guantanamo Bay.

X-Rays

The use of X-rays as life-saving diagnostic tools took a sinister turn during World War II when they were used to determine the fate of thousands. In pursuit of Hitler's master race, German medics travelled around taking X-rays of women of different nationalities to select those considered suitable to breed racially pure children. Slavic women, for example, weren't acceptable and were killed.

Dr Josef Mengele, who was dubbed 'The Angel of Death', and other doctors, conducted a range of abhorrent experiments in their relentless quest for genetic perfection. They tried X-rays, among other methods, to sterilise 'undesirable' women to prevent them from reproducing.

X-Shaped Cross

The X-shaped cross was known as the St Andrew's cross after the saint who was reputedly crucified on one. Andrew, the first disciple, considered himself unworthy to be crucified on the same type of cross used for Jesus Christ. Also known as the saltire, the X-shaped cross forms the national flags of Scotland and Jamaica.

Chilean torture victims reported being tied to an X-shaped wooden frame, with their genitals exposed for a severe beating.

YARDARM

217

Yardarm

Navy discipline was necessarily stringent. With a large number of men confined for months on end in harsh conditions, no breach of trust or violent behaviour could be tolerated without risking a loss of control. Mutineers, especially, were swiftly despatched to nip any unrest in the bud. Treason and desertion were the other two offences carrying the death penalty. However, it wasn't employed lightly as manpower was in short supply and it would have been foolhardy to have executed too many crew members.

When a serious offence was committed and the death sentence passed, the prisoner was hanged at the yardarm, usually at 8 a.m. the following day. He was walked to the prow of the vessel in front of the ship's company, his hands and feet tied together and a noose placed around his head. At the appointed time, his shipmates pulled sharply on the rope to swing the body up to the yardarm on the foremast in what was known the 'yard-arm dance'. It was by no means an instantaneous death and unless his mates jerked sharply on the rope, he died by slow strangulation. The body would be left for several hours before being taken down, wrapped in a hammock and buried at sea. Occasionally, a sailor would jump overboard to avoid such a horrible death.

Next to hanging, one of the worst punishments a sailor could receive was to be swung from the yardarm. As the vessel rolled in high seas, he could swing 50 to 75 feet each way – enough to make the hardiest salt seasick.

Sometimes a sailor was punished because he was so dirty, his smell had become offensive to his mates. They'd either stand him in a tub of seawater and scrub him down with stiff brooms, or else tie him to a board which was attached to the yardarm and give him a few duckings over the side.

Sailors were also dunked from the yardarm when the ship crossed the equator as part-punishment, part-ceremony and part-ablution.

Actor John Mills fondly recalls a punishment he received while on board HMS *Volage* during World War II when his gun crew neglected to cover the weapons while on their watch. They were sentenced to painting the yardarm, a tricky job given the location of the target. With brushes tied to their wrists and paint pots tied to ropes, they crawled gingerly along the spar to reach its full length. All was going well until one of them dropped the pot, covering the grey funnel below with black paint, so they had to paint that too.

ZERO
TOLERANCE

Zero Tolerance

A fittingly modern approach to punishment, zero tolerance is a desperate bid to make societies safer where the normal measures have failed. It's a far cry from the days when zero tolerance meant that no one escaped the brutal clutches of the law. Nor does it involve the drastic punishments of old when we burned people at the stake or flogged them for misbehaviour, but it does attempt to address a 21st century situation.

There aren't many towns in Britain where one can walk fearlessly at night, despite heightened public awareness and the installation of CCTV cameras. We have a huge problem with street crime – especially among young people – with few effective deterrents.

With the conviction that petty offences can lead to serious crime, New York's Mayor Rudy Giuliani launched a widely-acclaimed campaign of zero tolerance in the late 1990s, aimed at removing troublemakers from the streets of a city considered to be the most dangerous in the world. Under his 'get tough on crime' banner, every offence from prostitution to panhandling was prosecuted, resulting in an impressive 45 per cent drop in violent crime.

Birmingham, Alabama, has seen a dramatic

fall in its crime rate since the introduction of zero tolerance policies which focused particularly on drug offences there. US crime rates overall are at their lowest on record, with rapes, robberies and assaults falling by half.

In Rio de Janeiro, police have also declared war on the city's minor offenders, clearing the streets of beggars and homeless children and clamping down on thieves, unlicensed hawkers and unruly motorists.

Supporters of zero tolerance believe it's important to tackle all types of crime rather than only the most serious. The police, they say, have concentrated on crime and forgotten about order. The unchecked growth of antisocial or illegal behaviour has enabled serious criminals to move in and take over the cities' streets. Critics, though, say zero tolerance wouldn't work in Britain because it would invite police brutality and destroy community co-operation with law enforcement officers.